Do human rights travel?

Helena Kennedy, Massoud Shadjareh,
Heiner Bielefeldt, Christine Loh

With an introduction by
Saad Halawani

Series editor
Rosemary Bechler

First published 2004
British Council
10 Spring Gardens
London SW1A 2BN
www.britishcouncil.org

Cover design by Atelier Works

Contents

Preface
by the Director-General

The British Council seeks to build long-term relationships between people of different cultures. Our currency is trust. The British Council has been a leader in cultural relations since its founding in 1934. In order to celebrate our 70th anniversary, I asked Counterpoint, our think tank on cultural relations, to commission a series of ten sets of essays, each set looking at a central issue from a variety of angles and viewpoints. The issues range from European enlargement to 'Britishness', and from the significance of death to the role of faith and the nature of secularism.

The 34 writers come from all over the world, though at least one in each set is British. Each introduction, with one exception, is written by a member of British Council staff. They testify to the richness of the intellectual and moral resource that the British Council represents.

Our intention is to stimulate debate rather than arrive at consensus. Some essays are controversial. None of them expresses, individually, a British Council viewpoint. They are the work of individual authors of distinction from whom we have sought views. But collectively, they represent something more than the sum of their parts – a commitment to the belief that dialogue is the essential heart of cultural relations.

Dialogue requires and generates trust. The biggest danger in what is often called public diplomacy work is that we simply broadcast views, policies, values and positions. A senior European diplomat recently said at a British Council conference: 'The world is fed up with hearing us talk. What it wants is for us to shut up and listen.' Listening and demonstrating our commitment to the free and creative interplay of ideas is an indispensable pre-condition for building trust.

To build trust we must engage in effective, open dialogue. Increased mutual understanding based on trust, whether we agree or disagree, is a precious outcome.

David Green KCMG

Introduction

Saad Halawani

In December 1948 the *Universal Declaration of Human Rights* was launched. The main aim of this declaration was and still is to prevent a repeat of the horrors that had been witnessed in Europe in the previous decade. I am not going to delve into the issues of cultural relativism and imperialism that are the usual realm of those suspicious of the universality of human rights principles, but I am going to talk about being at the other end of the human rights debate, and why at a certain moment I feel let down by those international bodies and mechanisms put in place to ensure that the rights of all are being kept on an equal footing among all peoples of the globe.

I have spent the last four years working for the British Council supervising, implementing and monitoring human rights projects. Those last four years were not easy. They challenged my belief as well as those of many others in the existence of a functioning system to stop human rights violations from taking place. My work was with people from varying age groups, but the most difficult moment was always the one when a participant at an event would come up to me and ask: 'You always talk about human rights, our duty to respect those rights, and how we need to take them into consideration in our laws and lives, but it is really astonishing that no one in the world is ready to budge to stop the daily human rights violations that are taking place here! So how do you expect us to believe that we are considered on an equal footing with other world nations?'

We are talking here about a high level of awareness of human rights, of people surrounded by graffiti on the walls of refugee camps to the tune of 'Where are our human rights Mr Kofi Annan?', which surprisingly enough rhymes well in Arabic. This adds to the many questions that always come from people who will look at you with their eyes wanting to believe you, but who find it really difficult.

Looking at the current state of affairs, some of the world's inhabitants feel that principles of human rights must apply to a different species and not to them. You can see this in many parts of the world: Rwanda was an example; the killing and massacres in Bosnia-Herzegovina is another one; Chechnya stars in a category of its own; as well as Palestine, Turkey, Iraq, Tunisia, Colombia – and the list goes on. The degree of influence that the political opportunism of the international community has over human rights issues, in terms of determining when to intervene and when not, is frightening and striking. Some human rights activists were thrilled when NATO took action against Serbia and Montenegro during the Kosovo crisis, and started talking about a new era where military action could be used to suppress any human rights violations in any place on the face of the earth. What the activists failed to notice was that a crisis of such magnitude in the centre of Europe was such a destabilising factor that all means were used to calm the situation and bring the crisis to an end, without addressing human rights violations. Like all Palestinians, I am acutely aware of the extent to which UN resolutions and international law are either pursued with vigour or ignored and undermined, pretty well at the convenience of the most powerful members of the international community.

What we are seeing is a deterioration in the ethics of human rights so extreme that they may be used as a mere pretext for achieving political gains. No one in the international community showed real interest in stopping the massacres in Rwanda when they took place. All over the world military campaigns against civilian populations erupt against the background of varying degrees of concern from the international community, according to what political and economic interests are at stake. Those who violate human rights can rest assured that, with political backing provided and the might of a military machine, nobody will even dare to criticise them.

This is not to undermine the courageous efforts of organisations that keep track of these violations all over the world, or those national bodies that dare to stand up to their governments. These organisations need support to continue with their work, for frequently they will feel the whip of governments that want to exploit them in every possible way while making the funding of these organisations conditional upon taking certain positions or deviating from established policies.

Exacerbating these contradictions in which human rights workers live, political pressures to ignore realities on the ground make it difficult to do one's job. Repeated arrests and beatings at the hands of government agents are a continuous threat. But there is nothing worse than living among a population that wants to believe in you and in what you stand for, while you find yourself continuously undermined by the inaction of the international community when they are put to the test.

Add to this the challenge to those who work in human rights of the ever-changing terminology governments use to justify violations of human and citizens' rights, ranging from security and national interest, to internal affairs where no outsider should interfere, and simple denial. Human rights workers, left totally devoid of support against almighty governments, are often accused of following and implementing a foreign agenda or even treason. Human rights is one of the most volatile fields you can work in. The lack of internal support and the abundance of testimonies to the hypocrisy of the international community leave human rights defenders dangerously isolated. They struggle against the tide of ever-constraining measures in the name of combating terrorism on the global and national levels, but really have very limited space in which to see the seeds of their work grow.

For those who enjoy protection for themselves and their animals, human rights are very natural and seem normal. It would be unheard of for a European citizen to be arrested and held *incommunicado* for numerous years, or for a sweeping curfew to be imposed over the city of Bergen, say, on the basis of nothing but rumour. But for those whose rights are violated continuously, human rights pose such an irresolvable dilemma. They see a world that claims to protect these values, yet at the same time fails to intervene when needed, due to political considerations. It really forces them into a position where disbelief reigns. And sometimes, they wish that they could at least aspire to the same rights that animals have in other countries.

Are human rights universal?
Helena Kennedy

'It is better to risk being consigned to the hell reserved for alleged
Westernisers and imperialists – however unjustified such a
criticism would in fact be – than to stand around in the vestibule
waiting for a time when everyone will like what we are going
to say.'
Martha Nussbaum, *Sex and Social Justice*, 1999

In 2003, Shirin Ebadi was awarded the Nobel Peace Prize for her
work promoting human rights. A Muslim woman lawyer from Iran,
Shirin Ebadi has worked tirelessly to promote the rights of women
and children in particular, often without regard for her own personal
safety. It is her view that there is no conflict between Islam and
human rights or democracy. She uses shari'a law, upon which Iran's
laws are based, to argue that there is no legal foundation for rules
that discriminate against women and give them inferior status. Other
areas of the law have been freshly interpreted to adapt to modern
circumstances and she is confident that the same approach can be
taken with regard to women's rights. 'My problem is not with Islam,
it's with the culture of patriarchy,' she has said. 'Practices such as
stoning have no foundation in the Qur'an.'[1]

Shirin Ebadi's views and her powerful commitment to human
rights in the face of great adversity are immensely inspiring. She is
also a symbol of the universalism that many Western liberals advocate
and cherish. She is the personification of our belief that human rights
are indeed for everybody. She is a symbol of what is possible.

While her achievement is a cause for celebration among human rights activists in Iran and beyond, the response it prompted in her home country also provides a salutary reminder of the challenges that remain. Ms Ebadi's return to Iran after receiving her Nobel Laureate was met with chants of 'Hello freedom' from thousands of supporters gathered to mark her arrival. But the Iranian President, Mohammad Khatami, also had a message for her. 'Do we have to issue an official message about whatever happens in the country?' he said. 'In my opinion, the Nobel Peace Prize is not very important. Of course, the prize on literature is important, but the one for peace is not.' He said he hoped that the recipient would bear the interest of the Islamic world and Iran in mind, and 'not allow the position she has achieved to be exploited.'[2]

The universalism of human rights remains a hotly contested issue between governments, individuals and non-governmental bodies. It has always been a contentious issue, but the events of September 2001 and their aftermath have thrown those arguments into stark relief. It is necessary for all of us to examine the issues again. What makes us so sure that universalism is right? Can relativism be justified? And if we espouse universal human rights in theory, how can we make that a reality in practice?

Human rights provide us with a new language for discussing our relationships with each other and with the rest of the world. They offer us a language that belongs neither to the left nor the right, because it is non-ideological; and it can speak to all the peoples of the world, irrespective of religious belief, because it is avowedly secular. Human rights are, in a sense, an exposition and codification of what, as sentient moral beings, we feel that each person has a right to in life. They place justice, tolerance, mutual respect and human dignity at the heart of all our activity.

The essence of our contemporary understanding of human rights is contained in the great statements of rights of the late 18th century – in particular the American *Bill of Rights* and the French *Declaration of the Rights of Man* in 1789. Our modern understanding of rights owes much to these documents. Philosophers questioned the unthinking obedience to religion and the monarchy. Through a rationalising, scientific study of human social relations, they developed the idea of rights rather as we find them today. The fact that individual rights originated in the European Enlightenment has often been a cause for criticism from opponents of human rights, who argue that they are culturally specific and imperialist.

However, though human rights were developed out of Enlightenment ideas, the *Universal Declaration of Human Rights* was drafted at a time when those values were facing the greatest of possible crises. After 1945, in the still fresh fever of outrage and horror at the Holocaust, international law turned its attention to individuals, and the modern concept of human rights was unlocked. Never again would such atrocities seen. Individual humanity would be protected and individual responsibility for such egregious crimes, recognised. This was something entirely new and it had enormous potential. The drafting of the *Universal Declaration* was a specific response to the barbarity taking place in Europe and elsewhere in the 1930s and 1940s. So in a sense, the *Universal Declaration* was much less a celebration of the supremacy of Enlightenment values than a warning about how badly things can go wrong.

Moreover, drawing on this history, I would suggest that one of the best arguments in support of universal human rights does not relate to a theory of rights, but to the reality of what rights actually do for people, and, as Nazism demonstrated, what can happen to people when they are denied such rights. Human rights need to be rooted in the evidence of history, which has amply demonstrated that humans are at risk of their lives if they do not have some free agency. This must be upheld by internationally recognised rights entitling individuals to oppose unjust laws within their own states and, as a last resort, to enabling them to appeal to other nations and international organisations for assistance in asserting their rights.

Arguments based upon history are persuasive, particularly because they do not depend on a particular understanding of human nature. People from different cultures may continue to disagree about what is good, but may nevertheless agree about what is unarguably wrong. Sometimes it is easier to explain rights negatively: we all know that none of us want to be tortured or locked up indefinitely without trial or proper legal process. This can be a helpful way of fostering an understanding of the universal relevance of human rights. However, I think it is possible to go further. As Chair of the British Council I have been very privileged to visit many countries where I have met countless individuals working to promote human rights; I am also a criminal lawyer. The tales I have been told by the people I have met all have a common thread running through them. Invariably these are people who have been disenfranchised and discriminated against on account of their gender, their religion, their politics, their race, their skin colour, their sexuality or their age. They tell of their second-class status, their insecurity, their exploitation, their poverty, and their loss of liberty, livelihood and dignity. An abhorrence of such indignities and degradations strikes a chord in so many of us. It is this that makes the language of human rights compelling.

These experiences speak to me of a common humanity that crosses borders and cultures; a human dignity that the *Universal Declaration of Human Rights* seeks to protect. Drawing on such experiences and upon the moral codes of diverse societies and religions, has led some thinkers to argue that human rights are rightly construed as universal because they represent a collection of values that are shared across cultures.

While such views are deeply felt, to make an argument based upon human nature is extremely tricky, because it invariably leaves one open to the charge of relativism. None the less, I think it is possible to make a strong case for the universality of human rights along those lines. However, the arguments need to draw not so much upon what different societies define as values, but upon what capacities and needs define what it is to be human, and distinguish human beings from the animal world.

These are ideas that have been developed by Bhikhu Parekh, Professor at the London School of Economics and Political Science (LSE) and the University of Hull.[3] What he suggests is that there are some universal moral values that can be derived from an examination of the needs and capacities that all humans demonstrate, irrespective of their cultural origins. In looking at these needs and capacities he has articulated beautifully what it is to be human and has done so in a way that is consciously not culturally specific.

He says that humans have the capacity to 'understand, control and humanise their environment, make sense of their lives, imaginatively explore experiences, and develop ideas of truth, goodness, beauty and love. They create aesthetic, moral, spiritual and other values . . . they are also able to enter into meaningful relations with each other and create a world of deep attachments and loyalties that gives their lives moral and emotional depth.' Humans also have common desires and needs – 'they wish to live, desire food and physical wholeness, loathe disease and pain, require rest, need to remain active and seek sexual satisfaction'. Furthermore, they develop socially derived desires for self-respect, friendship and love and fear rejection and humiliation. They must be nurtured and, in order to form stable relationships and feel secure, they need a culture free from terror and complete unpredictability. And humans have an inner life that forms the basis of their subjective sense of the world.

These (and other) needs and capacities shape what it is to be human and as a consequence of them, people in all communities will have a number of features that are themselves specifically human. They include an ability to enter into meaningful relations with others;

the possession of capacities that are unique to humans and privilege them over animals; a capacity to create a world of meaning and values; and, as a result of common capacities and desires, the need for certain common conditions that allow them to survive and flourish.

Universal moral values are essential in order to protect these special human features, which themselves derive from those special capacities of humans unique to them. Bhikhu Parekh's list is not exhaustive, but he does identify five universal moral values: human unity, human dignity, human worth, the promotion of human well-being and equality. These values protect those things about being human that are so very exceptional. And when we think about the rights that are contained in the *Universal Declaration*, the convergence is striking. Those who drafted the *Declaration* may not have started by analysing human capacities and needs, but they could very well have done so. The text they agreed recognises those universal needs and capacities and, in doing so, draws on the values identified by Lord Parekh. This seems to me to make a very good case for the universality of human rights.

If there are strong arguments in favour of universalism in human rights, why does the concept meet with so much criticism? The main charges against universal human rights are themes I have already touched upon – cultural imperialism and the need to embrace cultural diversity, not universality. One of the difficulties with many of the criticisms of universality is that they do little to diminish the central claims of human rights theory. The insistence that human rights cannot be universal is often actually about something else altogether – sustaining structures of power that are authoritarian or patriarchal.

The first point to make is that the founding document for modern human rights discourse, the *Universal Declaration of Human Rights,* adopted in 1948, was the product of a meeting of a great diversity of minds. The star in the creation of the new legal order was

Eleanor Roosevelt, who chaired the first meeting to draft an international charter in February 1947. The declaration was not the result of a few meetings of Anglo-American and European lawyers. The commission responsible for drafting the declaration was described by one British official at the time as 'a rather wild and woolly body',[4] reflecting the fact that represented at the table were an immensely diverse group of people. The drafting commission had representatives from 18 member states of the UN including India, Iran, Egypt, Lebanon, the Philippines, China, Chile, the Soviet Union and Uruguay, as well as more predictably, France, the UK, the USA and Australia. Chaired by Eleanor Roosevelt, the commission's Vice-Chair was Ghasseme Ghani from Iran and the rapporteur was Charles Habib Malik from Lebanon. The many traditions and cultures represented among these people included Chinese Confucianism, Islam, Hinduism, Marxism, Catholicism and Middle Eastern Christianity. It was accepted that it was neither possible nor desirable to attempt to create a universal legal system. The idea was to create a template of agreed rights and standards against which all governments and legal systems should be measured.

So the founding document for the new human rights regime was painstakingly drawn up through an inclusive process of discussion and debate. Yet many of those who reject universal human rights castigate those who promote their universal adoption as culturally imperialist. This seems ironic, given that the impetus for the *Universal Declaration* was a broad rejection of Nazi imperial ambitions in Europe in the 1930s and 1940s. Moreover, while 'cultural imperialism' makes a nice soundbite, as an egalitarian concept human rights are anything but imperialist in their objectives. As a criticism of universal rights, this idea of cultural imperialism is a pretty flimsy reproach.

Human rights are anti-imperialistic in their intention. They seek to give a minimum level of power to individuals, which should allow them to challenge authority where appropriate and enable them to protect themselves against injustice. They are about ensuring that no one is treated in a way that would be harmful to a person's ability to meet his needs and make the most of his capabilities. They are about ensuring that power is not exercised over people in ways that those in authority would themselves reject if they found themselves among the powerless rather than the powerful.

Human rights also assume that individuals are best suited to determine for themselves what kind of life they want to lead, and what principles should guide it. In turn that implies that one should not be able to impose one's own vision of the life on another without their consent. The *Declaration* implies both a right to choose, and a right to leave.

Naturally, this is a threat to those who operate patriarchal or authoritarian systems. It particularly concerns me when criticism of universalism is essentially providing a cover to protect the power of elites in communities or states. It is essential to recognise that the rights of the individual are often the object of the exercise of power by others. This seems to be the case in relation to 'honour' killings, which occur where a woman is said to have brought dishonour on the family or community, perhaps by refusing a marriage partner, pursuing her education and career or because of suspicions of an affair. These are ways of exercising power over women, and if they dare not to comply, the consequences can be fatal. These murders happen all over the world – in Pakistan, India, Afghanistan, Albania, Iraq and Turkey for example, but also in the UK. Though not generally condoned, they are in some countries treated with leniency, and they are often covered up within families and by some members of a community. Though sometimes linked with Islam, they are neither an Islamic tradition, nor a specifically Islamic problem, since they happen in all kinds of communities. However, they are often not reported out of fear, and in some countries honour has been used as legitimate defence to murder. In Turkey for example, the government in July 2004 finally promised to introduce more serious penalties for these crimes – but in the past their punishment has often been lenient. Tackling this crime should not be used as an excuse for a thinly veiled racism or Islamophobia, but it must none the less be confronted, both in the UK (a process that has already begun in Scotland Yard) and internationally. Such terrible crimes cannot, and must not be justified by a resort to relativism. The push towards cultural relativism, which can sometimes seem inevitable, actually militates against the weak. As Michael Ignatieff has written, 'relativism is the invariable alibi of tyranny'.[5]

The criticism of universalism is a measure of how greatly leaders in some patriarchal and authoritarian societies fear for the fragile foundations of their power, since human rights do not seek to determine how people should live; they simply seek to allow people to choose. In some societies it will be argued that it is right for men to have power over women: strictly controlling who women can marry, who they can talk to and where they are allowed to go. These approaches to life are objectionable to most human rights advocates in the West. But the point of human rights is not to say that people cannot live in such a way *should they wish to*. Human rights do not seek to prevent people living life in their communities as they wish. The point is that the individual should be able to choose, freely, whether or not he or she wishes to live a life based upon those principles. Moreover, he or she should be allowed to opt out of such approaches to life without fear of punishment.

Individual-based rights in fact protect, rather than constrain, the cultural diversity that is so much prized by the anti-universalists. Without guarantees of the individual's right to choose how he or she lives their life, a society that permits many cultures would be impossible. Cultural diversity, about which many critics are so concerned, would be impossible. The accusation of rampant individualism fails to address the text of either the *Universal Declaration* or the *European Convention for the Protection of Human Rights and Fundamental Freedoms*. In both documents there are clear provisions protecting our ability to form and sustain the relationships that hold society together, encapsulated in rights relating to the family, religion and freedom of assembly. Article 29 of the *Universal Declaration* is explicit in saying that 'everyone has duties to the community in which alone the free and full development of his personality is possible'.

Indeed, we must not forget that what we are claiming is that human rights are universal – not absolute. Article 29 of the *Universal Declaration* is also important here, stating that an individual's human rights may be limited in order to secure due recognition and respect for the rights and freedoms of others. Likewise, there are few unconditional entitlements in the *European Convention*. Some rights, like freedom from torture, are absolute, but most involve a careful consideration of the rights of others.

A further irony is that those who reject universalism, are not usually prepared to endorse a culturally relativist approach towards the diversity within their own group. While they say that rights cannot be applied universally across cultures because of cultural diversity, they are often quick to claim a uniformity of values within their own culture, which they seek to defend. Shirin Ebadi, and her pursuit of rights for women and children, manifests precisely the kind of divergence of opinion within a culture that patriarchal, traditional societies seek to suppress.

Making the case for universalism can be particularly difficult in those circumstances where those who are the 'victims' of human rights violations actually condone the culture or community that legitimises the abuse of their rights. What should not be forgotten is that these individuals will often lack the resources – whether financial, educational or otherwise – to challenge the diminution of their rights. They may even consent, but this is perhaps because they do not have the resources to dissent, even if they wished to do so. In relation to women, Martha Nussbaum argues that the very injustice that deprives a woman in a deeply patriarchal society of some of her rights, may deny her the ability to imagine an alternative. Many women accept subjugation because to challenge the status quo is a frightening as well a liberating prospect.

Of course, no one is suggesting that human rights norms should not be interpreted differently in different cultural contexts. After all the whole idea of human rights recognises the significance of autonomy and the variations in practice that will often result. The European Court of Human Rights has developed a concept of the 'margin of appreciation' that allows some (limited) variation in interpretation between states. People in all kinds of places may experience similar difficulties and challenges in their daily lives, and it will be sensible to find solutions that will work in the circumstances in which they live. However, by no stretch of the imagination does that mean that ultimately the only solution that can work for any particular group is one that solely originates with that group. And it certainly does not mean that every element of every culture is to be accepted where the human rights of individuals are breached.

Some of the governments criticised for their failure to comply with international standards, reject their need to do so not on substantive grounds – that is, that the rights set out are wrong and should not apply universally – but on the grounds that human rights do not fit with the traditions of the people they govern. Yet there is no logical reason why something that is traditional is inherently desirable or ethically valid. Nor can it be argued that traditions are immutable and should be shielded from change.

What's more, we should look with scepticism at those traditions that apparently justify an abdication from human rights. Female 'circumcision', or mutilation, is defended on grounds of tradition in some African and Middle Eastern countries, yet it has nothing to do with Islamic doctrine. The promotion of tradition within a society too often turns out to be an instrument of power and control in the hands of those in positions of authority.

In making criticisms of universal human rights, some non-Western states tend to frame their criticisms in terms of the perceived hypocrisy of Western or US policy – for example, the USA is criticised for failing to take an even-handed approach in the Israeli–Palestinian conflict. As it happens, that criticism may often be justified (and I will come on to this later) but it is not in itself a criticism that is grounded in a culturally particular view of the world. It is not saying, 'we object to this approach because it is contrary to our tradition'. Rather it is saying, 'we object to this approach because you are operating double standards, which is unfair'. In fact, by criticising this hypocrisy, states are making a demand for equal treatment. In other words they are seeking a universal approach, which treats everyone fairly and equally.

The suggestion that universal human rights are a tool of Western imperialism or global domination suggests that human rights principles go unquestioned in those states that promote them with most vigour. A cursory examination of the facts demonstrates this is not the case. Protecting human rights is still a struggle in the West too. The language of rights applies not just to the abuse of others on the grand scale; it also relates to the small acts of inhumanity that disfigure the lives of people in the West. The idea behind human rights – respect for the essential humanity and moral worth of others – should be a thread running through all our human interactions – at home and in the workplace, in schools and hospitals, in the courts and in our political institutions. They should play a central part in our everyday lives – though too often they do not.

The UK government sought to address this with the enactment of the Human Rights Act in 1998, which gives the government and public authorities human rights responsibilities. Great praise is deserved for this decision, but it should not be assumed that this means the government is unequivocal in its adherence to human rights. Human rights have proved a fertile area for legal debate and legal challenge and the government is frequently put to the test by cases brought against it where individuals have sought to establish their rights under the Human Rights Act. Cases about privacy and freedom of speech – particularly those involving celebrities – have received much publicity in the press. But there have been countless other cases. In June 2004 the Human Rights Act was used to establish that, just as the surviving partner in a heterosexual relationship is entitled to take over a tenancy when his or her spouse dies, so too can the surviving partner in a gay relationship. Human rights have been invoked in cases about the treatment of prisoners and conditions in prisons, in employment cases and in cases concerning the right to life. Human rights are likewise at issue in the question of whether a Muslim girl should be free to wear a headscarf or a *jilbab* (a long, flowing gown) to school. These issues have been prominent in the UK, but also in France, where headscarves and any other religious dress have been banned – on the grounds of the strictly secular nature of the state. I firmly believe that women should be allowed freely to choose how they wish to dress. In all these cases, there is sometimes broad consensus about how human rights should be protected, and at other times a debate that is vigorous and divided.

What we see in these debates is not so much a challenge to the universality of human rights, but an impassioned debate about what those rights mean. The fact is that if human rights are a challenge for some non-Western governments, they are equally a challenge to those governments in the West that are seen to be leading the imposition of universal human rights.

There are many ways that we can refute the arguments against universality, but however good the theory is, universality also needs to be demonstrated in practice.

It is extremely damaging when human rights become a camouflage – or appear to be a camouflage – for a less honourable political motive. As a human rights advocate, it was particularly depressing, in all the hubris surrounding the war in Iraq in 2003, to hear the rhetoric about freeing the Iraqi people from the tyranny of Saddam Hussein – a claim that seemed to act as a smokescreen when the original case for war began to look a little thin. To use the language of rights expediently cheapens it. It discredits the governments that use such rhetoric and it discredits the very cause of human rights.

The struggle to create binding international norms is further undermined when the United States and other Western states refuse to accept constraints on their own behaviour. Disregard for the human rights of others by those countries that have been most prominent in their promotion – most obviously in Guantánamo Bay and Iraq – further weakens the case for universalism.

It has been a source of great shame to people in the UK and the USA to see the abuses of prisoners taken in the war in Iraq. The image of the Iraqi prisoner, standing on a box, hooded, arms outstretched, with wires apparently attached to his arms and his testicles, was almost iconic in its visual power. It will, I have no doubt, come to be a symbol of this shameful episode in 21st-century history. The incarceration of prisoners in Guantánamo Bay without even a semblance of legal process prompts similar disquiet, though a decision of the US Supreme Court in June 2004 that those held at Guantánamo were entitled to invoke the US courts' authority just as any US citizen can, looks set to bring about necessary change.

In the UK, the indefinite detention without trial of non-UK citizens under the Anti-terrorism, Crime and Security Act – introduced in 2001 after the events of September 11 – has likewise been an affront to the rule of law and human rights. These powers could be introduced only if the UK derogated from Article 5 of the *European Convention on Human Rights,* which protects the individual's right to liberty. The government justified this move by claiming that there was a terrorist threat to the UK that amounted to a public emergency, which was a threat to the life of the nation. This was a view that did not go unquestioned, not least by parliament's Joint Committee on Human Rights. The impact of this approach is similar to the impact of Guantánamo Bay – it leads people to ask why there is one law for some and a different law for others. It is the antithesis of universality, and it can only damage international relations in the long term. There cannot be a hierarchy of human rights.

The points to draw from these developments are not complex, but they are important. First, they demonstrate that human rights are not a done deal anywhere. Their universalism is most widely accepted in the West, but Western governments are not beyond reproach in their actions. They do not come with clean hands to the marketplace of ideas. But second and most importantly, while I recognise that pragmatism is sometimes necessary in international affairs, Western governments must be conscious of the damage they do by failing to follow the principles they expound. Meanwhile, we must not allow ourselves to forget that human rights remain political; there will always be battles to fight and it is unlikely that there will ever be a time when vigilance will not be necessary.

While there is so much that threatens to undermine universality we need to find more effective ways of promoting it. Probably the best way to promote universality is to talk less about the theory, but engage more actively in the practice, and in particular that means cross-cultural dialogue and discussion. Through transnational collaboration on substantive issues, there is far greater potential to do good, which is after all what human rights are all about. I feel very pleased to say that in this respect the British Council has a particularly significant role to play. As a generally trusted and respected organisation the British Council can work on human rights issues, providing people with the resources and space to understand their own situation and to explore the options that should be open to them. A few examples illustrate how this can work.

In 2003 the British Council ran a project in Jordan looking at family protection. This was a taboo-breaking initiative in Jordan – an unprecedented development in a largely patriarchal Middle Eastern society. In Jordan, domestic issues are traditionally closed to any discussion outside the family – let alone intervention. This project enabled the country's officials to discuss and prevent violence and abuse against women and children for the first time ever, bringing together judges, politicians, the police, NGOs and even religious leaders. Unprecedented reforms followed, including the preparation of a draft law to provide shelter services for female victims of violence. For the first time the government of Jordan was saying to the public that it would not tolerate the abuse of women's rights and would assert the role of the state in protecting them.

In east and central Africa a project to help women politicians develop leadership skills had a tremendous impact both on the British and African participants. An exchange programme was set up between women politicians from east and central Africa and women MPs from the UK. Women from Eritrea, Ethiopia, Kenya, Malawi, Tanzania, Uganda and Zambia visited the UK and spent time shadowing British MPs in parliament and in their constituencies. Following these visits a number of UK MPs made a return trip to visit their exchange partners. For both groups the experience was an opportunity to learn about the challenges faced by women politicians in very different situations and to share ideas and strategies. Although the economic situation and political cultures from which the MPs came were very different the exchange participants were surprised to identify many common themes and experiences. The women from east and central Africa were particularly surprised to discover how common domestic violence was in the UK. The Hon. Alicen Chelate from Kenya explained: 'I thought this was a problem in Kenya because of culture and tradition but I have come to see that it is a problem in the UK and for women all over the world.'

I have taken up a good deal of this essay refuting some of the arguments of the relativists and refuseniks. This is a necessary task. The arguments against universal rights are in most cases poorly made and do not stand up to scrutiny. There is an important issue about diversity, but it cannot, in my view, ever justify a resort to relativism when the rights of women and children, the excluded and the dissenting are at stake.

The promotion of universal human rights around the world is justified not because patriarchal or traditional authority is oppressive or uncivilised by the standards of the West, but because it is oppressive and uncivilised by the standards of those who are the objects of its tyranny. But perhaps what is more important than anything is to support actively those who are working to develop a culture of human rights in their country – both governments and individuals, such as Shirin Ebadi and the thousands like her all over the world. While I will not hesitate to advocate the universalism of human rights, I know too that they will have the deepest roots if they come from within, rather than being imposed from without. Individuals want to find their own voices and shape their own destinies. We have a duty to support and encourage, where possible, the individual's right to live life according to his or her own ambitions and dreams, without living in the shadow of a fear of violence or ostracism. Rights have to be given the force of law because this is how we link our dreams to the acts of daily life. Everyone should have the opportunity to do just that.

Endnotes

[1] Cited in *The Guardian*, 12 June 2003.

[2] Cited in *The Guardian*, 15 October 2003.

[3] See his essay 'Non-ethnocentric universalism' in *Human Rights in Global Politics*, Tim Dunne & Nicholas J. Wheeler (eds), 1999.

[4] See A. W. Brian Simpson, *Human Rights and the End of Empire*, 2001, p. 363.

[5] Ignatieff, *Human Rights as Politics and Idolatry*, 2001, p. 74.

Bibliography

Ken Booth and Tim Dunne (eds), *Worlds in Collision*, Basingstoke, Palgrave, 2002.

Michael Freeman, *Human Rights,* London, Polity, 2002.

Fred Halliday, *Islam and the Myth of Confrontation,* London, I. B. Tauris, 1996; 2003.

Michael Ignatieff, *Human Rights as Politics and Idolatry,* Princeton, Princeton UP, 2001.

Helena Kennedy, *Just Law,* London, Chatto & Windus, 2004.

Martha Nussbaum, *Sex and Social Justice*, Oxford, OUP, 1999.

Bhikhu Parekh, 'Non-ethnocentric universalism' in *Human Rights in Global Politics*, Tim Dunne & Nicholas J. Wheeler (eds), 1999.

Geoffrey Robertson, *Crimes Against Humanity*, London, Allen Lane, 1999; 2002.

A. W. Brian Simpson, *Human Rights and the End of Empire*, Oxford, OUP, 2001.

Whose rights are they anyway?
Reaching a critical understanding of human rights-speak in the 21st century

Massoud Shadjareh

Bandirma Prison sits two hours across the Bosphorus from Istanbul. As bleak as any prison, its inmates are split into two categories: criminal and political. In 1998, two colleagues and I visited Turkey, to see for ourselves the state of civil society in a country hailed before and since as an exemplar to the Islamic world: a modern Muslim democratic nation state.

Accompanied by two local activists (one now in exile, the other serving 15 years for being part of an 'illegal' organisation) we met several political prisoners. One in particular started me thinking about this game we play called human rights advocacy. Sat either side of layers of perspex and iron grill, I spoke with a journalist who is serving various sentences for writing articles on Islam, the Kurdish situation and non-violent, pro-Palestinian protest. What he had to say to me left me shocked.

He was a victim of torture – a serial 'offender', in the sense that he had been tortured and imprisoned before for making comments and writing his newspaper articles. But the idea of us advocating on his behalf, as a man whose rights to free speech and political dissent had been violated, was anathema to him. 'Don't spin me as a human rights case,' he told me, without any rancour. 'That's not what I am.'

This has to be the most chilling indictment of human rights regimes that I have faced first hand. Here was a man whose toenails have been extracted in a bid to make him recant his political views; who feels so alienated from traditional human rights discourse that he actively did not want his advocacy to be conducted via the mechanisms either of law or theory that have become so familiar to us.

It is easy to deride his derision as an inept and culturally relative response to enlightened universalism – the charge of 'particularism', or even 'chauvinistic exceptionalism' so readily levelled at everyone from Richard Rorty to Ayatollah Khomeini, and from critical race feminists to the non-aligned movement. However, I am about to argue that we global civil society activists need an honest reappraisal of the human rights project as we encounter it, as a deeply flawed discourse, if we are to salvage any hope of moving towards global community and understanding between peoples.

This is not an academic essay – it is a view from the ground. Without over-generalising, we need to look at the theory of universal human rights hitherto, the implementation of law upon this basis and the working of human rights organisations within the context of a burgeoning global human rights community. Each of these elements, under scrutiny, yields fresh clues as to why human rights are resisted as a concept. However, they also throw us lifelines – ways to salvage a universal concept of justice in theory, practice and law that may not provoke the revulsion of those most in need.

Problems with the origins of universalism

As eloquently noted by Mary Ann Glendon, the *Universal Declaration of Human Rights*, the founding document of the human rights movement 'is already showing signs of having achieved the status of holy writ within the human rights movement'.[1]

The case of the Turkish journalist is continuing, and may be very near an amnesty, so I will call him 'Ali' for now. Ali would be commonly termed an Islamist. Already a pejorative idiom back in 1998, it is now almost synonymous with 'terrorist' in media and social parlance. Taking his basic frame of reference as Islamic texts, Ali is bracketed, perhaps bucketed would be a more accurate description, into the various categories of pre- or post-modern particularism and Muslim exceptionalism, along with Osama bin Laden, the Taliban, Saudi Arabia and probably (had he been a Muslim) Cardinal Richelieu. This is despite the fact that one of Ali's sentences is for an article in which he declares that it is an Islamic duty to fight for oppressed people, which in the Turkish context specifically translates into talking about the Kurdish situation, regardless of whether those oppressed are adherent to Islam, any religion or none.

There are writers and thinkers like Abdullah An-Naim[2] who regard Islam, and more specifically shari'a, the aspirational legal system many Islamists seek, as an archaic monolith that needs rigorous interrogation in the light of modern standards of human rights.

Ali and his ilk, motivated by many religious affiliations or none, are likely to contest this approach. Looking at the narrowness of consultation that marked the drafting process of the *Universal Declaration of Human Rights (UDHR)*, might they not be justified in their charge that this is no less a culturally particular or even parochial document, doomed to eternal exclusivity, than any religious text, as viewed through a purely anthropological lens?

The *Universal Declaration* is so strong on many issues, so imperative in its assertions and so inviolable in the eyes of its adherents that it takes a brave man (and it is a gendered document to the extent that it takes 'man' as its reference point) to query its norms, even to the extent of needing further interrogation. A place to start, however, might be the purely 'Western' legal and theoretical specialisations of its ethnically diverse but basically uniform drafting teams. We are referred in the document's pages to *The Rights of Man* and the New Testament. But where are the references to the Qur'an, and *Das Kapital*? Even the USSR's presence during the process was struck out in many places when their representative turned out to be a low-ranking employee from one of the embassies or consulates. That was an irregularity. Clearly his impartiality would have been undermined by this position: a conflict of interests might ensue. Impartiality, as defined by this project, was well served by the role of the project co-ordinator, Eleanor Roosevelt, whose husband had only just left the White House.

This is a horribly cynical view of the origins of the *UDHR*, and it pains me to write it. But this is how many see it, and those many include writers, activists, individuals and groups who are at the core of what human rights discourse should be about, that is, the victims of some of the most atrocious human rights abuses around the world. Often, but not solely, Muslim, these people are discounted as having a poorly developed sense of individualism that invalidates their critiques.

The universalists among us pooh-pooh their concerns in less than helpful ways, habitually regarding them as postmodern rehashings of destructive communalist ideas. Let us assume for a moment that feminism in all its disciplines is a rights-based discourse, and look at the critique of a universalising feminist standpoint from the point of view of critical race feminists. To Kathleen Neal Cleaver or Adrien Katherine Wing, for example, the equation of white women's experiences with those of women of colour is a fallacious, not to mention racist, practice. Any empirical analysis of American society will turn into a table of shame for women of colour who are at the bottom of every column charting 'equality' and high achievement, whether it concerns economic mobility, single parenthood, domestic violence, or a whole other set of classifications, which themselves are subjective and deeply flawed units of analysis.

To critical race feminists, it is, as Rorty says, solidarity between oppressed communities and those who wish to see an end to oppression that promises a *modus operandi* for a better and more just world. This argument for equality and parity between communities, ideologies and individuals is a seductive analysis that gathers many followers.

Universalists en garde! Perhaps, it is charged, these critics are too wrapped up in a defensive sense of community to understand their obligations as part of a universal community of rights holders. Perhaps critical race feminism is the expression of a community of individuals who are, effectively, nothing more than bad losers.

But such charges are themselves an indictment of universalism's own cultural parochialism. As Makau Matua and others have pointed out, part of the pathologisation of the victims of human rights abuses involves their description as underdeveloped and savage. Just as we have created a hierarchy of rights in the *UDHR*, placing individual civil and political rights above economic and social rights, so we are prone, in our criticisms of anti-universalists, to patronise the positions of those whom we should respect. Worse still, we subjugate them in a normative hierarchy where your position at the top marks you out not only as morally superior (a rampant prejudice in itself), but it does so with the implication that this is the result of your own superior reasoning. Sandra Harding is brutal in her belittling of critical race feminism, Islamic feminism, certain feminist anthropologies et al:

> 'As several feminist literary critics have suggested, perhaps only those who have had access to all the benefits of Enlightenment can "give up" those benefits.'[3]

So there is a dividing line between *what* can and can't be criticised and *who* can and can't criticise. Are we witnessing the emergence of a new form of blasphemy? But might we not rather imagine that those who respond by criticising the *Universal Declaration* and the theories and law it has spawned, do so not simply to reject universalism in favour of multiple, equally valid discourses, but in an attempt to renegotiate terms. Might it not be the case that they do this so that everyone can move forward, towards a new and more comprehensive universalism; one that is properly cognisant of its limitations and its fallibility? This is Ali's contention when he says to his Muslim audience, that it is a religious duty to stand up for your oppressed brother, even if they are atheists. Islamist – maybe. Chauvinist? No. Universalist? Yes.

In short, it comes down to a question of theory – theories indeed – and whether these theologies, ideologies and anthropologies are all equally up for grabs. Are we engaged in an equal re-evaluation, or are we risking normative development by allowing a recalcitrant chauvinism to dress itself up as a universal rights discourse?

One rule for 'them' and one rule for 'us'

'The Court found that the University of Istanbul's regulations imposing restrictions on the wearing of Islamic headscarves and the measures taken to implement them were justified in principle and proportionate to the aims pursued and, therefore, could be regarded as "necessary in a democratic society".'[4]

The panoply of human rights law should be something to celebrate in a world that has emerged from the horror of holocausts and genocides in Europe. However noble, its symbolism and standards belie a grating reality that for the peoples of the world is not 'one size fits all'.

As we write, the European Court of Human Rights (ECHR) has made a decision likely to set back the cause of universalism for decades, entrenching in society and European law what had formerly been a crude stand-off between Muslims in Europe and the idea of human rights.

Finding in favour of a diktat set in law by a government whose all-powerful military is always looking over its shoulder, the court accepted Turkey's defence that its ban on the *hijab* – headscarves for Muslim women – was 'a democratic necessity'. Putting aside the many defects in the court's reasoning, this will have a monumentally negative effect in polarising identities between Europe and its Muslims. These processes, the triumph of mutual stereotyping, could well have been averted by the intervention of what has increasingly been promoted as the ultimate arbiter of conflict – human rights discourse. A check against rampant ideologies, whether they are theological or secular, human rights discourse as it manifests itself in legal processes for individuals at the ECHR level, set out to protect (or at least try and protect) the weak and the oppressed from the vagaries and vengeance of the state. But here, the ECHR's ruling has cast the expression of personal faith in the role of villain and the all-powerful state as hero.

The judgement finds that there has indeed been state interference in the freedom to practice one's religion – a *prima facie* human rights violation – but that this was justified, since it protected the religious rights of others (other students at Turkish universities who would not now feel compelled to wear a scarf thanks to the display of this headgear by another student); also, that it was a check against the rise of religious fundamentalism threatening to undermine democracy. As an added insult, the ruling concludes that such a ban ensures equality between the sexes – a highly subjective, indeed prejudiced finding.

Many Muslims in this situation have been criticised for what is perceived to be their newly discovered interest in rights-speak, on the basis that this concern is extended on behalf of Muslims in minority situations only, and is not shared across nations, religions and crises. There is some truth in this. Many Muslim campaigns, communities and individuals are guilty of this charge. So too however, are many others belonging to an '-ism' or '-ology' of other kinds.

Michael Ignatieff has pointed out that those who support the rights of one group against another that oppresses them do not always worry about the rights of those that compose the oppressor group. Turkey again provides a useful example. While the Refah Party and its subsequent incarnations used rights-speak to protest the ban on its activities and even existence, it failed to make mention at any stage, in and out of government, of the torture, abuse and cultural persecution of Kurds by successive Turkish governments. Somehow, we have to get beyond the idea that rights have values that allow one group to prevail over another, whoever they are – oppressed or oppressor, European/Western over Islamic/Southern or any other.

Finally, the Leyla Şahin v. Turkey case also entrenches in legal precedent the growing perception among global cultures that there is one law for them ('them' being the developed, Westernised world) and one law for us. It seems to mark as well and truly over, the pretence that in theory and in law, the post-war human rights regimes are universal.

Issues around the trial of Saddam Hussein and his cronies, confirm this message. Well rehearsed already are the claims that a legal process has been politicised, used by an American occupation force to legitimise a US-appointed regime left in its wake. Others charge that it is to diminish Saddam's crimes to allow him to go on trial at a national level, when those crimes were indeed crimes against humanity. In the interests of a final justice for all those victims of Saddam's crimes, people are moreover concerned, as they should be, that he himself should get due process; and that the fairness of his trial (not entirely assured at the moment) helps draw a line under the spiral of injustice in Iraq.

What has been little discussed, however – itself a revealing sign of prejudice – is that the monumental war crimes committed by his forces against Iran during the 1980s, including his possession and use of chemical weapons, do not figure among the many crimes Saddam has been charged with. According to a leading Iranian human rights organisation, The Organization for Defending Victims of Violence (ODVV), there are still 100,000 chemical veterans in Iran. Figures for those soldiers and civilians who were either killed by chemical weapons, or indeed survived them, are under compilation. Why then, the argument goes, should we raise our sights beyond our own rights, when the prevailing international order does not recognise us as sufficiently human to benefit from current human rights law?

The same argument is used by the Palestinian suicide bomber. As human rights activists, we sometimes fail to understand that what seems to us to be the most savage and barbaric of acts is seen by the perpetrators and their supporters not so much as an act of martyrdom as one of justice. Justice, not revenge. Why? Because for every crime committed by the Israeli Defence Forces or ordered by the Israeli government, there is no effective framework in international law that can be used by a Palestinian to seek redress. Whether you look at the International Court of Justice, the International Criminal Court or the Security Council, a Palestinian whose house has been demolished, who faces destitution and humanitarian distress on a terrible scale, is failed by human rights law.[5]

How do we negotiate this stark failure? It has to begin with those of us who promote the idea of everyone being equal under the law, recognising its abuse and its limitations. A Palestinian or Israeli or for that matter Tamil or Sinhala, or Catholic or Protestant based in Northern Ireland may never accept his foe, either as individual or community, as a part of his shared value system. Any of them may well argue cultural relativism. They have a right to do so, as long as this does not involve the brutal treatment of other individuals and cultures. However, they, and the millions worldwide for whom international law is an irrelevance, can and will continue to justify their relativism by invoking its inconsistent track record.

Activism and organisations: help or hindrance?
It has often been noted that today's human rights activists operate in the same way and with the same zeal as the missionaries of empire two centuries ago. It is a depressing thought that the human rights activism of today may be so mired in hypocrisy and the blood of unjust wars fought in the name of human rights from Afghanistan to Iraq, that we should give up on a universal project.

The dilemma is exemplified by the experience of an acquaintance of mine who formerly worked for a leading international human rights NGO. Starting a campaign for an imprisoned Turk who brandished a Qur'an at a former president, he found himself castigated by activists who thought the imprisonment justified, or the prisoner, by his religious association, was not a fit subject for their activism. This is the worst form of supremacist exceptionalism, lightly done as are so many other similar acts, by sleight of hand in the name of norms. It is a sad fact that Islamophobia and many other xenophobic prejudices operate unexamined within the human rights community.

It was something that we at the Islamic Human Rights Commission (IHRC) experienced first hand in the early days of our operations. One of our first campaigns was for the release of Mu'allim Ibraheem Al-Zakzaky imprisoned by the junta of Sani Abacha in Nigeria from 1996 to the end of 1998, for making the statement that: 'There is no authority except through God.' Not only he, but many of his followers from the Muslim Brothers, were imprisoned, raped or killed by Abacha's police and army. There was no difference between their harassment and that of other anti-Abacha activists except that (a) they were Muslim and adhered to an Islamic rather than national identity, and (b) they were raped, killed and imprisoned in much larger numbers than any other group.

This was not recognised in human rights reporting at the time. When the Muslim Brothers were mentioned in the documents of IGOs it was as part of a ubiquitous 'Islamic threat'. There are complex reasons for this exclusion from the agendas of human rights organisations, not least because those persecuted felt alienated and therefore did not prioritise making their case known to the human rights community. Much of this was soon overcome when we began bringing their situation to light through more conventional processes, that is, media releases, action alerts and all the other paraphernalia that characterises human rights campaigning. However, there were many examples in this particular campaign where prejudice to the point of exclusion prevailed.

We submitted a report to the Commonwealth Secretariat highlighting the plight of Al-Zakzaky and others (as had been suggested to the campaign by the then British Foreign Secretary Malcolm Rifkind) and then found ourselves holding a vigil outside the gates of Marlborough House while Commonwealth officials and various NGOs discussed Nigeria's future. Our leaflets demanding, 'Free Al-Zakzaky' were aimed at the general public but we found them being picked up by participants at the conference as they left for lunch. On their return many governmental representatives and human rights NGO officers came over and began asking about the cases we were highlighting. One NGO officer suggested we submit a report to the Commonwealth so that it would be distributed at meetings such as the one we were protesting about, and we would also be invited to participate. He was duly surprised to learn that we had already submitted extensive, well-documented reports. We remained uninvited, and worse, the reports were not disseminated. According to the delegates we were meeting, some of whom had little knowledge of Nigeria other than what the papers handed out at the meeting, Sani Abacha was the ugly face of Muslim prejudice bearing down on a large section of Nigeria's population because of their Christianity. A 'more' Muslim stance it was presumed, could only be much 'worse'.

This was in 1997. One of our initial projects had been to launch a website. Thanks to this, our report was downloaded by delegates that day and used later in the meeting. The internet helped us get the message out far and wide in a way that was a monumental step forward at the time, although now it is taken for granted. Al-Zakzaky had visited and lectured in the UK many times before. But when he came in 2001, he was widely sought after. He could not meet with every media outlet or NGO or community that wanted an interview, a lecture or a visit.

What was gratifying was not his 'celebrity' but the fact that he had been acknowledged as someone who had been vilified and attacked for his beliefs, and that he was worthy of the same attention as 'conventional' prisoners of conscience. Al-Zakzaky had been imprisoned a total of nine times by various Nigerian regimes since 1979. His last stint was the first time he has been acknowledged as a prisoner of conscience.

Up until the last days of his imprisonment there was still mainstream resistance to advocating for 'Islamists'. A long-time campaigner on Nigeria, based in Malaysia, e-mailed us at the end of 1998 informing us of an interview he had heard on the BBC World Service, where the UN's Special Rapporteur was questioned about Nigeria prior to his visit. According to him, Nigeria had by that time released all political prisoners and he was happy with this new-found respect for human rights. 'What about Ibraheem Al-Zakzaky?' responded the interviewer. Thrown by the question, the Rapporteur promised to investigate as soon as he landed in Nigeria. A fortnight later Al-Zakzaky was free.

Those two years of campaigning saw a sea change in the way such cases were viewed, but also a change in the characterisation of human rights activism. By the end of that period no one ever thought twice about including our submissions regarding Nigeria in their own reports. IHRC's journey from pariahs to participants is a success story, but it is also a disheartening reflection on the institutionalising of prejudice in the systems that should work to dismantle them. Our exclusion – and we have felt it since then also – is based on our religious convictions. On paper it makes no sense and seems ridiculous. In practice it is having devastating consequences for those defeated by this exclusivity.

Currently in the UK, we face a situation where successive waves of anti-terrorist legislation since 1997 have made synonymous first 'terrorist' and 'Islamist', and now arguably 'Muslim' and 'terrorist' Every kind of activism from leafleting to demonstrating is now a cause for concern when their perpetrators are Muslim. 'Innocent until Proven Muslim' was the title of an article written by a colleague five years ago about Yemen. It might be applied just as well to the UK now. A new form of internment created by the Anti-terrorism Crime and Security Act 2001, has an unspecified number of Muslims stifling under 23-hour lock-downs in Belmarsh high security prison – not even two hours from the Houses of Parliament. Charged with nothing, they are detained upon suspicions now proven in some cases to have been formed from intelligence gained through torture confessions by various secret services. No basic rights for these Muslims then. When we did this to the Irish some 30 years ago, we created a whole new class of men who had been at worst Republican supporters and who, upon their release, enrolled into the ranks of the paramilitaries. Belmarsh houses two types of prisoners: the criminal and the political.

Meanwhile on the streets, various police forces are operating an unofficial policy of 'Muslim profiling' where a beard or a scarf or just the look that you are possibly Muslim makes you more likely to be stopped and searched now under various laws, particularly anti-terrorist laws. It is a humiliating experience, and we have had cases reported to us of civil servants being stopped by armed police and searched Hollywood-style in Whitehall; and a Labour member of the House of Lords has been stopped and searched twice; one of our colleagues – a white, middle-class, NGO activist – was pulled over while driving to the office. The policemen were very nice, and she joked with them about whether they pulled her over because she was a white, middle-class woman, or because she wore a headscarf and was obviously Muslim.

If the nightmare of a monumental terrorist atrocity in London comes true, God forbid, British Muslims (of which almost a million reside in the capital) are as at much risk of being maimed and killed as anyone else. Yet they are considered solely as a threat by the security police. The proposed extension of indefinite internment to British nationals (according to the Home Office, to iron out the discriminatory anomaly that currently exists) is no joke. We can pray for the nobility of those who endure this kind of suffering, but we shouldn't hold our breath. It is simple. If you differentiate between yourself and others, others will differentiate back.

Coda

But truly universalist alternatives do exist. Those alternatives include the defiance of Israelis, Palestinians and other internationals who are members of the International Solidarity Movement in Palestine; and the determination of 'Ali' who is not a pacifist, but definitely is a universalist, now in an F-type high-security prison somewhere else in Turkey.

These two examples admittedly symbolise vastly different visions of universal values, which would then seem set up to fail, much as our current human rights regime does. However, the fact that people can exist who co-operate with others not sharing their vision, whether they are Islamist, pacifist, whatever they are – this surely lights the way to moving beyond all those essentialist notions of human rights activism, and those the activists choose to advocate for. Their philosophies need to be brought to the negotiating table, together with the myriad others excluded thus far in what increasingly appears to the truly dispossessed, as a rule of might in the name of human rights.

In order to address these issues, whether it is the hierarchy of rights or notions of gender and equity, everyone has to be able to contribute, even if it is only the decision not to contribute after all, to the development of a more universal human rights agenda that realises its limitations. This opens the way, moreover, for the ultimate prize, the fantastic potential of engaging those in most need of assistance, not simply as the passive recipients of a benevolent human rights process, but as active participants in and creators of the way forward. Every time we exclude someone from participating in this discourse on the basis of their (perceived) particular interest, we create yet another victim of human rights abuse – that is, someone who has been denied the opportunity to express their agency as rational beings.

Endnotes

[1] Makau Mutua, 'A Third World Critique of Human Rights'.

[2] See e.g. *Toward an Islamic Reformation: Civil liberties, human rights and international law,* Syracuse: Syracuse University Press, 1990.

[3] Quoted in Miller, Nancy 'Changing the Subject: Authorship, Writing & The Reader,' *Feminist Studies/Critical Studies,* T. de Lauretis (ed.), Indiana University Press, 1986.

[4] Press release issued by the Registrar, European Court of Human Rights, 'Chamber Judgments in the cases of Leyla Şahin v. Turkey and Zeynep Tekin v. Turkey', 29 June 2004.

[5] See *Bringing Israel to Account,* Uzma Karim, London: Islamic Human Rights Commission, 2004.

Human rights in a pluralist world

Heiner Bielefeldt

Human rights claim universal validity: this is a truism. The *Universal Declaration of Human Rights* adopted by the United Nations on 10 December 1948 refers in its preamble to 'the inherent dignity and . . . equal and inalienable rights of all members of the human family', demanding that human rights serve as 'a common standard of achievement for all peoples and all nations'. Article 1 of the Declaration asserts that 'all human beings are born free and equal in dignity and rights'. The UN World Conference on Human Rights, held in Vienna in June 1993, not only confirmed 'the universal nature of these rights and freedoms', but claimed it to be 'beyond question'.[1] One could cite copious UN documents in which this claim to universal validity receives clear and unequivocal recognition.

And yet, it is also true that the universalism of human rights has often been, and continues to be challenged. Among the various objections raised by critics and sceptics, three arguments stand out. First, human rights are seen as an exclusive *manifestation of Western culture*. It is implied that since the concept of human rights emerged historically in Europe, its inherent universal validity claim amounts to a modern form of cultural imperialism. The second argument is based on the assumption that human rights are essentially *individualistic* and hence incompatible with the more communitarian ethical spirit of some non-Western cultures. Third, since the very notion of human rights is predicated on an *anthropocentric focus*, it is argued that a priori, human rights are inapplicable to people or cultures who cherish a theocentric or cosmocentric worldview. I would like to offer a reading of universal human rights that can respond to these three main objections.

I will be dealing here with the concepts involved in the normative claims of human rights, rather than the many important questions of political and legal implementation, or the various instrumental ends and purposes to which, as we can all too often observe, governments on every continent subject human rights.

A Western heritage?

Human rights: a Western construct with limited applicability – this is the slogan of cultural relativism in general as well as the title of an article by Adamantia Pollis and Peter Schwab. The authors argue that since human rights originated in Western Europe and North America they remain inexorably linked to certain philosophical concepts in the Occidental tradition; and that therefore, upholding the universal nature of human rights is either a self-deluding act, or a more or less aggressive form of cultural imperialism. This argument may be the most popular objection against the universalism of human rights in general. Certainly, it has been promoted over the years by numerous journalists, politicians and scholars of different disciplines. Its most famous recent proponent is Samuel Huntington in whose global map of civilisations human rights are located exclusively in the West.[2] Ironically, Huntington's ethnocentric position seems to be shared by quite a few non-Western critics of universal human rights who also subscribe to the view that the claim of universality simply conceals particular Western values and interests.

What makes this type of reasoning *prima facie* all too persuasive is the fact that the genesis of human rights concept indisputably took place in the West. The concept combines three components – that is, (1) the *universalistic claim,* (2) the *liberating spirit* and (3) the connection to *juridical (or quasi-juridical) implementation mechanisms* – clearly first developed in the writings of European lawyers,

43

politicians and philosophers. It was in Western countries, moreover, that the idea of human rights first gained political momentum, gradually becoming a cornerstone of the political identity of liberal democracies from the late 18th century onward.

Let us agree to assume that historically, human rights developed in the West. However, this assumption still remains open to different interpretations. From the multiplicity of possible interpretations, I would like to contrast two major approaches that I call the *cultural essentialist interpretation* and the *normative constructivist interpretation* of the history of human rights. These two readings have very different systemic consequences for our understanding of their universality.

The *cultural essentialist* line of *interpretation* tends to see human rights as 'rooted' in the Occidental tradition at large. It is no coincidence that many of its advocates actually turn to the Bible (that is, both the Jewish Bible and the Christian New Testament)[3] as one of the roots – or even *the* root – of the idea of human rights. Above all, they cite the book of Genesis, according to which the human being has been 'created in the image of God' and has thus been endowed with an inalienable dignity. Another useful reference is Psalm 8, which praises God for having accorded the human being a special rank within the whole of creation: 'Thou hast made him little lower than the angels, and hast crowned him with glory and honour.' From the New Testament one can quote St Paul's proclamation from Galatians that 'there is neither Jew nor Greek, there is neither bond nor free, there is neither male nor female: for ye are all one in Christ Jesus'. Reference has often been made to the writings of ancient pagan philosophers, too, especially those from the Stoic school of thought. One may think, for instance, of Marcus Aurelius who teaches that all human beings constitute but one family united not by physical bonds of blood and seed but rather by their common participation in the divine *logos*.[4]

Now, the cultural essentialist interpretation of human rights contends that the development of human rights should be understood as originating from these and other cultural 'roots' of the West. The 'root' metaphor further implies that the history (or pre-history) of human rights can be described as the process of a (more or less organic) 'ripening' of what has eventually led to a fully fledged concept of human rights. In this line of argument, the Protestant Reformation, the Western Enlightenment and other periods of historical transformation appear as important steps within that evolution, whereby essential humanitarian messages first contained in the Bible, in Stoic philosophy and other Western sources, received further clarification, and more consistent practical implementation. Finally, the ripening process is said to have culminated, in the late 18th century, in the various declarations of human rights both in North America and Western Europe.

Within this line of argument, because it is assumed that what is 'rooted' in a particular tradition basically belongs to that same tradition, it naturally follows that human rights constitute an exclusive part of the Western cultural heritage. The root metaphor suggests that human rights remain *essentially connected to a particular cultural 'territory'*, that is, the very territory in which their roots first gained ground. It goes without saying, according to such an interpretation, that unless people from non-Western cultural backgrounds are ready to adopt Western culture (or at least important parts thereof), they cannot have full access to understanding and enjoying human rights. To turn once more to the root metaphor, the recognition of human rights outside the West thus seems possible (if at all) only as the process of a – voluntary or involuntary – *implantation* of achievements whose cultural roots basically lie in the West. It can be no surprise that people from non-Western cultures often show reluctance to espouse a system of values that has undergone such a more or less thoroughgoing 'Occidentalisation' process.

Unlike the essentialist interpretation, the *normative constructivist interpretation*, to which I subscribe,[5] does not deny that historically, human rights first developed in the West. But it does give a very different account of that development. Rather than the result of an organic cultural ripening process, human rights are considered to be the *specifically modern product of incomplete learning processes* brought about, above all, by political crises and conflicts.[6]

What triggered these conflicts historically was *experiences of injustice*, such as the devastations caused by religious and civil wars in early modern Europe, systematic abuse of state authority in the age of absolutism, social insecurity in the wake of modern capitalism, the occupation and exploitation of foreign lands by European colonial powers, or threats to human dignity by modern data processing or genetic engineering. To be sure, horrible experiences of injustice run through every seam of human history. What is specifically modern, however, is that new communication technologies help to expose better the *structural causes* underlying such atrocities. Whereas under pre-modern circumstances, injustice was typically considered as originating from the moral shortcomings of local masters and rulers – that is, personal failures best addressed by moral and religious edification – modern communication technologies have opened up new avenues for comparing the problems that people are more or less similarly confronted by in different countries. This has given rise to analysis of the underlying causes of injustice, as well as common political and legal strategies designed to overcome such problems.

One other aspect of modernity may be even more important for the understanding of human rights. That is, in the modern era people have increasingly found themselves in a condition of *radical pluralism*: people of different worldviews, political and ethical affiliations, religious or non-religious convictions literally live, and have to live, side by side. Again, it would be wrong to suggest that pluralism *per se* is a completely new phenomenon. However, whereas traditional models of shaping religious and cultural pluralism such as the

Ottoman Millet system, were based on the juxtaposition of discrete collective entities, the mobility and volatility of modern life implicate us in a much more direct daily confrontation with people of a different belief system or forms of life. In this situation of increasing pluralism it becomes more and more difficult to shape societal coexistence normatively by simply resorting to the unquestioned authority of collective values, customary laws, predominant religious traditions or a shared understanding of what a good life means.

Human rights offer a basic insight – a way of coming to terms with the challenge of radical pluralism that modernising societies face today all over the world. That is, *pluralism itself* should be appreciated and welcomed as something positive, namely, an expression of *human freedom,* which itself points to the *dignity of every human being as a morally responsible subject*. In other words, the crisis of traditional forms of ethical and legal consensus gives rise to a new – and admittedly more abstract – search for consensus, based on the recognition of everyone's equal freedom and dignity, which is to be respected and protected in terms of binding rights. This insight – the guiding principle of human rights – is foregrounded in Article 1 of the *Declaration of Human Rights,* as quoted above, which continues: 'All human beings are born free and equal in dignity and rights. They are endowed with reason and conscience and should act towards one another in a spirit of brotherhood.' The various articles of the *Declaration,* which range from freedom of religion and expression via the rights of democratic participation to a number of social rights, constitute a catalogue of rights, where the guiding principle of the equal dignity and freedom of every human being is spelt out in detail.[7]

It does not follow from the fact that the idea of human rights, as far as we know, first emerged in Western countries, that they are essentially and eternally confined to the cultural heritage of the West.[8] Unlike the cultural essentialist interpretation, the *normative constructivist reading* of the history of human rights primarily draws on *experiences of injustice and their structural causes in modernising societies*, experiences which, to a large extent, people today share all over the world. From the outset, from this perspective, the normative responses to that challenge first spelled out in the West, are relevant to people living in other cultural settings, too, wherever they struggle for justice. This does not mean that the Western history of human rights is the binding model that people in non-Western societies are simply supposed to adopt. What it does mean, however, is that the experiences and reasoning processes underlying the development of human rights in the West can be, in principle, 'translated' into other cultural contexts. To be sure, in both interpretations, culture plays a role. But the metaphor of *translation* as opposed to *implantation* marks the basic difference between the constructivist and cultural essentialist understandings of the history of human rights.[9]

The possible *translation* of the basic insights underlying human rights cannot take the form of a one-way communication from 'the West to the rest'. Instead, it should lead to *communication in all directions,* opening up opportunities to gain new perspectives on how to further develop human rights, as well as how to make the existing system more consistent and more effective.

Equally clearly, the learning process prompted by such an idea of universal human rights remains *unfinished*. Since its beginning, it has been a learning process in which not only *failures of practical implementation* but also *bias in the prevailing articulation* of human rights have been critically addressed, for instance, by abolitionists, feminists, trade unionists or spokespersons from anti-colonialist movements. It continues to be a process to which people from different cultural contexts can *actively contribute*. That its tenets were first coined by lawyers, philosophers and activists, in the West, loses much of its saliency in the face of this continuing dynamic. In any case, the equation of human rights with essentially 'Western values' can no longer be justified.

However, the normative constructivist reading of human rights, which I advocate, is not 'post-traditional'. It does not do away with all reference to particular cultural traditions. Rather, what counts is *how exactly* this reference is made. For instance, for a devout Christian it is natural enough that Biblical motifs, such as the status of the human being as an 'image of God', or other elements of the Christian tradition, will co-resonate whenever human dignity and human rights are in dispute. This is a good thing, because reconciling modern human rights claims and religious tradition allows the person to embrace human rights as something that fits together with the cultural or religious foundation of their personal identity. However, one has to be aware that the appreciation of human rights, say, from a Christian background, should not lead us to confusing human rights with exclusively 'Christian values'. Maybe there is only a thin line between an *appreciation of human rights* from a particular cultural or religious tradition on the one hand, and an *essentialist appropriation of human rights* by that tradition on the other. But it is all the more important to preserve that line.

The same holds for other traditions, too. Take the example of Islamic interpretations of human rights. Again, it is one thing to appreciate human rights from a Qur'anic perspective and to discover possible analogies, say, between the moral force inherent in human rights and the demands of justice laid down in the Qur'an. But it is a completely different thing to derive human rights in an essentialist way from certain Qur'anic verses, thereby claiming an exclusive 'Islamic heritage of human rights'. A number of specifically 'Islamic human rights declarations' manifest exactly this strongly essentialist tendency. They absorb the idea of human rights into an exclusively Islamic framework, in such a way as to totally obscure their universal nature.[10] Generally speaking, one should be anxious to make sure that the perfectly feasible and rewarding, appreciation of human rights from the standpoint of different religious or cultural traditions, does not lead to forms of 'essentialist occupation' in which the idea of universal human rights could eventually get lost in competing closed sets of cultural or religious values.[11]

An expression of individualism?

Critics who challenge their universal validity, also typically invoke the individualistic nature of human rights. They assume that there is an unbridgeable gap between individual human rights on the one hand and cultures in which an ethics of communitarian solidarity predominates on the other.

Take Bassam Tibi, who holds that the concept of individual human rights is essentially opposed to the Islamic doctrine in which he says 'the individual is considered a limb of a collectivity, which is the *umma*/community of believers'. Mohamed Jawhar has identified the same source of antagonism. He writes: 'Islamic order is built around the community, not the individual.' Jawhar refers us to the communitarian spirit of his country, Malaysia: 'Islam's emphasis on the community is echoed as well in pre-Islamic Malay values, which stressed that the paramount obligation of the person is social, first to his family and then to his community.'[12] One could easily find more quotations to illustrate that widespread tendency of playing off individual rights against communitarian solidarity and vice versa.

Closer analysis, however, shows that human rights and communitarian ethics are far from incompatible. No doubt, the stress placed on human rights as individual rights is justified in that they indeed aim to protect each individual person. Human rights do allow for the 'trumping'[13] of individual rights *against* state and community. At the same time, it should be noted that human rights also protect the person against enforced exclusion *from* society or community, such as, for instance, exclusion from democratic participation or arbitrary deprivation of one's citizenship. What ultimately counts in the context of human rights is not an abstract individualism but, rather, the *facilitation of freedom*, a freedom that cannot unfold unless it covers both the individual as well as the communitarian aspects of human life. Besides protecting the individual from unjustified interference by others, human rights therefore attempt to shape society at large in such a way as to promote *liberal community building* – in marriage and family life, religious communities, economic and cultural associations as well as political parties and international NGOs.

To give some examples, religious liberty not only entails the right of individuals to hold and express their religious convictions, but also comprises the right of religious *communities* to organise themselves in accordance with their own doctrines and to participate actively in societal life and public debates. Further, freedom of expression operates both as every individual's entitlement and as a precondition of *public political discourse* in a democratic society. Rights of cultural minorities necessarily have a strong communitarian aspect, although – *qua* human rights – they always at the same time protect the rights of individuals to shift or change their cultural allegiances. These examples may suffice to demonstrate that individual human rights are from the outset meaningfully connected with claims of communitarian solidarity. In fact, commitment within the various communities that make up a modern civil society is an expression of that principle of equal dignity and freedom that lies at the very core of the human rights idea.

From such a comprehensive perspective, the individual's (negative) right to preserve some independence *from* society or community should not be played off against the (positive) right to associate oneself *with* a community and participate in society at large. Instead, they form two sides of the very same coin, so to speak, in that they contribute to the possibility of *liberal community building*. Hence, on closer investigation, the frequently invoked abstract antagonism between individual rights and communitarian solidarity ultimately proves superficial and utterly false. The critical front line drawn by human rights does not run between 'the individual' and 'the community'; instead it runs between *liberal communities* (and societies) on the one hand and *authoritarian collectivities* on the other.

What is at issue in human rights is the free development of people – individually and within communities and societies – as opposed to all forms of authoritarianism. That is, human rights clearly are in opposition, for instance, to family structures based on enforced marriage, religious communities that threaten violence against 'heretics' and 'apostates', or political regimes without freedom of the press. At the same time, human rights also find themselves in contradiction to the pursuit of pure market economic policies, especially if such policies seem to accept mass unemployment as the unavoidable 'collateral damage' of economic reform strategies.

Anthropocentric bias?

The charge that human rights lead to an atomised society devoid of communitarian solidarity often goes hand in hand with the portrayal of human rights as reflecting an 'anthropocentric' philosophy, opposed to theocentric or cosmocentric world views. Cross-cultural debates on human rights, especially between representatives from Western and Islamic countries, have often focused on the purported antagonism between anthropocentrism and theocentrism.

No doubt, human rights can be called 'anthropocentric' insofar as they rest on a due respect for human beings. It is obvious that the only 'bearer' of rights, strictly speaking, is the human being who thus constitutes the very 'centre' of politics and law in the context of human rights. Such political and legal anthropocentrism, however, does not preclude religious – that is, 'theocentric' – interpretations of the moral spirit of human rights. Again, what counts is exactly *how* the theocentric perspective comes into play.

Anthropocentrism and theocentrism fit together as long as it is clear that they constitute different dimensions and thus belong to different levels of discourse. When it comes to shaping a political and legal order based on human rights, it is obvious that such an order in itself must be strictly anthropocentric. Claiming theocentric authority in the field of politics and law, that is, an authority that directly stems from God, inevitably leads to political authoritarianism, which would be clearly in contradiction to human rights. As a matter of fact, authoritarian regimes have frequently invoked 'divine rights' in order to limit or completely deny the legitimacy of human rights. Such a way of playing off divine against human rights can be observed to the present day.

But there are also other routes to a theocentric perspective. In liberal theological reasoning the notion of 'divine right' can be used to provide a symbolic foundation for the inalienability of human dignity, a dignity that requires respect and protection in terms of human rights. The Protestant theologian Jürgen Moltmann, for instance, takes such an approach. In his opinion violating human rights finally amounts to denying 'God's right with respect to the human being'.[14] In Moltmann's interpretation the concept of a 'divine right' is not used to limit the sphere of human freedom. Rather the notion of 'God's right' points to the moral and religious significance of human freedom as vested in the dignity and responsibility of every human being.

Comparable ideas have also been presented by some contemporary Muslim thinkers. For instance, Mohamed Talbi holds that Islamic monotheism requires the unequivocal recognition of religious liberty, including the right to convert from Islam to another religion, a right unknown to the traditional schools of Islamic law. In Talbi's view, violating a human being's religious liberty means to commit a major sin, that is blasphemy, by challenging the sovereignty of God who *alone* has the right to decide about the individual person's spiritual destiny. Thus, for Talbi 'religious liberty is fundamentally and ultimately an act of respect for God's sovereignty and for the mystery of His plan for man. Finally, to respect man's freedom is to respect God's plan. To be a true Muslim is to submit to this plan.'[15]

The frequently invoked general antagonism between anthropocentrism and theocentrism has no philosophical basis. What human rights, due to their *liberating spirit*, do preclude is *authoritarian forms of theocentrism*, such as theocratic regimes. However, the critique of religious authoritarianism can well gain support from liberal theological reasoning. In that context the 'theocentric' perspective may become an additional motive for fighting political abuses of the divine name, and setting up a political order centred around the mutual recognition of human beings in their equal dignity and freedom.

Conclusion

Responding to some typical objections to the universal nature of human rights, I have argued that even though human rights were first articulated in the West, their inherent normative force remains open to being appreciated from different cultural and religious (including non-religious) perspectives. I have further demonstrated that the stress placed on individual rights does not contradict communitarian values, because by protecting the individual person, human rights at the same time aim at facilitating liberal community building. Finally, I have argued that the political and legal anthropocentrism indeed presupposed in human rights, can easily be reconciled with an encompassing theocentric appreciation for the liberating spirit of human rights. To conclude, I would like to stress once more that human rights epitomise the respect that all human beings owe each other. Hence they cannot and should not be claimed as an exclusive heritage of any particular culture. If the language of 'heritage' is to make any sense at all, human rights can only belong to the *common heritage of humankind.*

Endnotes

1   Universal Declaration of Human Rights, 10 December 1948, G.A. Res. 217A
    (III), 3 UN GAOR (Resolution, part 1). Vienna Declaration and Programme of
    Action of 25 June 1993, quoted from *Human Rights Law Journal,* 1993, p. 353.

2   See Adamantia Pollis and Peter Schwab, 'Human Rights: A Western
    Construct with Limited Applicability' in same authors, (eds), *Human Rights:
    Cultural and Ideological Perspectives,* New York: Praeger, 1979, pp. 1–18, and
    Samuel P. Huntington, *The Clash of Civilizations and the Remaking of World
    Order*, New York: Simon & Schuster, 1996, pp. 70–72.

3   Although the Bible stems from the Middle East, it is nevertheless frequently
    invoked as one of the main sources of the 'Occidental tradition', alongside
    ancient Greek philosophy, Roman law and other sources.

4   Cf. Marcus Aurelius Antoninus, *The Communings with Himself*. Revised text
    and translation into English by C. R. Haines, Cambridge/Mass.: Harvard
    University Press, 1987, p. 335: 'And thou forgettest how strong is the kinship
    between man and mankind, for it is a community not of corpuscles, or seed
    or blood, but of intelligence. And thou forgettest this too, that each man's
    intelligence is God and has emanated from Him . . . '.

5   Cf. Heiner Bielefeldt, *Philosophie der Menschenrechte. Grundlagen eines
    weltweiten* Freiheitsethos, Darmstadt: Wissenschaftliche Buchgesellschaft,
    1998.

6   Cf. Dieter Senghaas, *Wohin driftet die Welt? Über die Zukunft friedlicher
    Koexistenz,* Frankfurt: Suhrkamp, 1994, p. 112: Human rights are
    'achievements brought about in long-lasting political conflicts during the
    process of modernization in Europe. They are by no means the eternal
    heritage of an original cultural endowment of Europe'.

7   The 1948 *Universal Declaration* marks only the starting point of the early
    history of human rights, which has already yielded a large number of legally
    binding human rights conventions including (more or less efficient)
    implementation mechanisms.

8   The Indian philosopher Sudipta Kaviraj criticises such an essentialist attitude
    towards human rights with the following argument: 'While the idea of
    subjects as bearers of rights only existed in a sketchy fashion in pre-modern

European history, a specific historical trajectory has developed these ideas into the modern conception of a civil society and civic rights. Indeed, one danger of reading this too far back into the European past is that this encourages essentialist thinking. The achievements of civil society are then associated with a mysterious and indefinable feature of European culture or 'Western spirit', which proves before the debate has begun that it is beyond the cultural means of other societies to create similar institutions.' Sudipta Kaviraj, 'Universality and the Inescapability of History. How universal is a declaration of Human Rights?', in Hans May and Sybille Fritsch-Oppermann, (eds), *Menschenrechte zwischen Universalisierungsanspruch und kultureller Kontextualisierung. Loccumer Protokolle 10/93*, Rehberg-Loccum: Evangelische Akademie Loccum, 1993, pp. 75–96, at p. 81.

[9] To give a practical example, by fighting for the rights of political dissidents, Nobel Peace Prize-winner Shirin Ebadi does not just apply a 'Western' concept (as an advocate of essentialism might contend) but rather refers to experiences of injustice in her own society, the Islamic Republic of Iran. The same holds for human rights defenders across all countries, cultures and continents.

[10] An example of this essentialist tendency is the declaration of *Human Rights in Islam*, adopted by the foreign ministers of the *Organization of the Islamic Conference*, at the 1990 annual session of the OIC held in Cairo. The central role of the Islamic shari'a as both the frame of reference and the guideline of interpretation of the Cairo Declaration manifests itself throughout the document, especially in its two final articles which state: 'All the rights and freedoms stipulated in this Declaration are subject to the Islamic shari'a' and, 'The Islamic shari'a is the only source of reference for the explanation or clarification of any of the articles of this Declaration.' Quoted from *Conscience and Liberty. International Journal of Religious Freedom*, 3rd year, no. 1, spring 1991, pp. 90–95.

[11] For a closer analysis, see Heiner Bielefeldt, '*Western* versus *Islamic* Human Rights Conception? A Critique of Cultural Essentialism in the Discussion on Human Rights,' in *Political Theory*, vol. 28, 2000, pp. 90–121.

[12] See Bassam Tibi, 'Islamic Law/Shari'a, Human Rights, Universal Morality and International Relations', in *Human Rights Quarterly* 16, 1994, pp. 277–99, at

p. 289 and Mohamed Jawhar, 'Cultural Traditions, Good Government and the Universality of Human Rights', in May and Fritsch-Oppermann (eds), op. cit., pp. 97–107, at p. 99.

[13] Ronald Dworkin, *Taking Rights Seriously,* Cambridge/Mass.: Harvard University Press, 1977, at p. XI.

[14] Cf. Jürgen Moltmann, 'Theologische Erklärung zu den Menschenrechten', in Jan Milic Lochman and Jürgen Moltmann (eds), *Gottes Recht und Menschenrechte,* Neukirchen-Vluyn: Neukirchener Verlag, 1976, pp. 44–60, at p. 45.

[15] Mohamed Talbi, 'Religious Liberty: A Muslim Perspective' in *Conscience and Liberty* 1991/I, pp. 23–32, at p. 31.

Culture clash: Asian political values and human rights
Christine Loh

'To have the kind of democracy Britain or America has developed, you need certain cultural impulses in a people . . . but China has always had an autocratic centre . . . you cannot break out of your culture altogether . . . culture is very deep rooted.'
Singapore Senior Minister Lee Kuan Yew

'The concept of human rights is a product of historical development . . . it is closely associated with specific . . . culture, and values of a particularly country.'
Liu Huaqiu, Head of Chinese Delegation to the World Conference on Human Rights, 1993

What are the cultural impulses that shape how Asians look at democracy and human rights? What are the important aspects of their civilisations that created those impulses? Is there a conflict of values between East and West? Since a civilisation is a cultural entity embodying the overall way of life of a people that involves values, norms, institutions, modes of thinking and behaviour, and not a political entity, it may contain more than one political unit. Those units may be city states, federations, confederations, or nation states, all with their own political systems.

Many people in Asia are said to owe most of their cultural values to Chinese civilisation. With its size and long history, China has always had a substantial impact on the rest of Asia. With the rise of China now as a world power, it is becoming important for the rest of the world to understand its cultural impulses because they affect China's behaviour on the world stage. At the same time, it is equally urgent for China to understand the values that drive other cultures and nations, as China becomes part of a global world where constant mixing can lead to greater understanding as well as conflict.

China's style of political behaviour can be traced back to its Confucian and imperial traditions, as well as the more recent practices derived from Marxism–Leninism–Maoism. In this essay, we will contrast China's political values and culture with those of the West in the area of democracy and human rights.

China scholar Lucian Pye once commented that China is a civilisation pretending to be a state. Today, more accurately, there are five distinct political entities within Chinese civilisation – Mainland China, Hong Kong, Macau, Taiwan and Singapore. These are predominantly Chinese societies. Currently, possibly Hong Kong and Taiwan are having the greatest impact on Chinese civilisation in terms of stretching the perimeters of political thinking, since much of the debate about democracy and human rights arising from these two regions introduces new ideas into mainstream discourse in Mainland China and even Singapore. Indeed, the discussion around democracy and human rights in these areas is a dynamic one, although it has a distinctive Chinese flavour. This is not to say that the Chinese or Chinese thinking have to be approached differently from all other sources of human thought, since many of the issues they are dealing with are far from unique in the world.

Chinese political tradition

The Chinese political tradition projects the perfect ideal of a benevolent central authority that rules with wisdom and compassion, thereby maintaining a great harmony between the ruler and the ruled. In accordance with this tradition, open political debates and processes have had little role in Chinese politics. Whether Confucianist or Communist, the Chinese have always believed that government should be guided by ideology and orthodoxy. In the past, government was justified by its exercise of 'benevolence'. Law existed to underpin political and social order. At present, government justifies itself by following the 'correct line' and leadership of the Chinese Communist Party (CCP), where the law is an instrument of state. This tradition has been in longstanding denial of the view that politics involve the clash of values and alternative ideologies. In such a system, truth resides with authority, and form often becomes more important than substance. Even today, differences among the political elites in Mainland China are still essentially settled behind closed doors; the secrecy that surrounds decision-making is hard to penetrate.

Traditional Confucian thinking put government at the core of Chinese civilisation: the most exalted task for man was devising proper and just government. *The Analects* of Confucius (551–479 BC) and the *Discourses* of Mencius (373–288 BC), another significant political thinker, constituted part of imperial China's essential learning on statecraft that candidates for civil service examinations were tested in up until 1905. The demands of good government in the Confucian ideal involved not only dealing with the problems of rulers but also creating a sense of cultural and political unity for all members of society through the pursuit of harmony. Thus, for centuries, there has been a stress on continuity and orthodoxy within Chinese politics. Politics was seen not as dynamic but static. Official thinking was not disposed to accept incompatible views and rivalry.

In China's long history, where duty was predominant, and society's principal business was government by the elite within a strict hierarchical system of authority, those involved in government had to display servility to their superiors in order to survive. The notion of 'small' or 'limited government', so popular today in the West, would have been extremely hard for the Chinese to understand. The issue of the political accountability of the sovereign was addressed by the concept of a 'mandate from heaven' or 'heaven's will'. When a dynasty collapsed, it was explained that 'heaven' had withdrawn from the sovereign his right to rule as a consequence of long years of poor governance.

Public and private institutions have traditionally been well integrated and made compatible within the hierarchical realms of Confucian thinking. Everyone supposedly knew his place within the great order of things and his relationship with superiors and rulers. Even today, non-state institutions in China, including religious bodies, are autonomous only up to the point allowed by the state. Thus, individuals and groups did not seek autonomy but rather greater connection with the state and those with political power. Self-sacrifice for the state was considered a great virtue.

Remarkably, the Chinese imperial system lasted till 1911, although the weakness of the Qing Dynasty compared with Western powers became obvious after the Opium War (1839–1842) as a result of which Hong Kong was ceded to Britain. This war represented much more than a trade war over an illegal product. It signalled the clash of the traditional world order of imperial China and the international order of nation states that had emerged in the West. When China was forced to open itself to trade, cede territories to the West, and discard its sovereign and judicial authority over foreigners in China, the concept of the mandate of heaven was fatally affected – a breach which eventually led to the end of the dynastic system.

The impact of the West created a sense of dissatisfaction among the Chinese. Chinese intellectuals began to debate the form of government that China needed to be strong and modern. Early reformists, such as Sun Yat-sen (1866–1925), envisaged a form of democracy as the necessary means to building up a strong state. By 1905, with the end of the imperial examination system, the study of Confucianism had lost its practical value. Sun argued for and founded a new republic to replace dynastic rule. He formed the Nationalist Party and was the republic's first president, which abandoned the Confucian political order that had guided China for centuries. Nevertheless, China's Confucian culture had an important influence on how the people–government relationship was seen even among the reformists, who often looked at the relationship between the individual and the state through a Confucian lens. They viewed democracy not as a way to emancipate the individual, but as a tool to consolidate state power, so that democracy and individual rights were seen as vital sources of national strength and power only because they could weld the ruler and the ruled into a single, cohesive whole to resist further foreign encroachments.

Human rights: universal v. culturally specific

Attitudes to state power in Mainland China today remain heavily influenced by traditional thinking and behaviour. The state remains all-powerful. Individual rights as spelled out in the Chinese Constitution are more akin to licences revocable by the state. The notion of rights is quite different in the West, where human rights are seen as 'natural', 'inalienable' and 'inherent' in every person, and laws are provided to constrain government and politicians. These notions, arising from Ancient Greek and Roman ideas of natural law and democracy, were strengthened by liberalism in its modern form, which began to take shape in the late 17th and 18th centuries. Political philosophers like Thomas Hobbes (1588–1679), John Locke (1632–1704) and Jean-Jacques Rousseau (1712–1778) based their writings on the natural state of man. Although each of these philosophers had a distinct notion of man's natural state, which in turn led to separate theories of ideal government, they all adhered to the idea that the state must justify its encroachment on man's original freedom. The Western liberal tradition has not always been seen in a favourable light in China even in modern times, particularly when liberalism was counterposed against Maoist ideology. One of Mao Zedong's (1893–1976) most famous essays is entitled *Combat Liberalism,* where he argued: 'Liberalism stems from the selfishness of the petty bourgeoisie . . . Liberalism is a manifestation of opportunism and conflicts fundamentally with Marxism.' It was to 'combat liberalism' that Chinese leaders sent troops into Tiananmen Square on 4 June 1989. Confucianism was also officially condemned in Maoist China as feudal thinking. While the ideas of Marxism–Leninism were Western imports, Maoism had a distinctive Chinese character.

Up until the 19th century, the Chinese language did not have words for 'liberty', 'rights' or 'human rights'. The word 'liberty' or 'freedom' in Chinese has been translated as *ziyou*, which literally means 'follow oneself'. The Western conception of liberty is some times said to appear to the Chinese as a recipe for 'chaos' and 'instability' where everyone does what they want. The Chinese word for 'rights' is *quanli* (power and benefit), and for human rights is *renquan* (people's power). The notion of 'right' first arose in the 1860s in the translation of Western works on international law. Chinese discourse on human rights since the 19th century has debated whether the various notions of rights and human rights should be seen from a collective or individual perspective. In the 20th century, the debate among scholars has moved closer to assigning rights to individuals although the collective view remains strong. The collective perspective on human rights was adopted by the nationalists, who relocated to Taiwan in the 1940s, as well as the communists, who established the People's Republic of China in 1949.

The rights discourse needs to be seen within the context of modern Chinese history. From the mid-19th century to the mid-20th century, China suffered foreign conquests, experienced the breakdown and eventual end of imperial dynastic rule, witnessed two world wars, and lived through civil war and revolution. It should not come as a surprise that there was a great compulsion among the Chinese to achieve stability and create a functioning government that could put the country back on the track to modernisation. Even at the end of the 20th century, the collective perspective on rights, duties and responsibilities remained the politically correct view. It was argued that stable politics and government provided the overall stability essential for economic and social development. In arguing its case today, China relies on a materialistic rather than a traditional Confucian approach.

The current official Chinese view on human rights is summed up in this 1993 address given by Liu Huaqiu:

'The concept of human rights is a product of historical development. It is closely associated with specific social, political, and economic conditions and the specific history, culture, and values of a particular country. Different stages of historical development have different human rights requirements. Countries at different stages or with different historical traditions and cultural backgrounds also have a different understanding of and practice in human rights. Thus, one should not and cannot think of the human rights standard and model of certain countries as the only proper one and demand all countries to comply with them.'

Liu's statement contained two theses: first, that cultures and countries have different concepts of human rights, and second, that there should be no demand for countries to comply with human rights concepts that differ from those in their own cultural traditions. The Chinese government's view is important because if it is held to be correct or is widely accepted by governments around the world, then the UN *Universal Declaration of Human Rights (UDHR)* would be much weakened. The *UDHR*, adopted in 1948, was a response to the horrors and devastation of the First World War. It marked the first international effort to secure 'the inherent dignity and . . . equal and inalienable rights of all members of the human family'. It supports a wide array of human rights, ranging from the most basic, such as freedom from slavery, to democratically elected government, and even an entitlement to paid holidays.

The Chinese government published a White Paper entitled *Human Rights in China* in 1991 in the lead up to the 1993 UN World Conference on Human Rights, in Vienna. The White Paper stated that: 'It is a simple truth that, for any country or nation, the right to subsistence is the most important of all human rights, without which the other rights are out of the question.' Although China has largely solved the problem of subsistence, the Chinese government believes that 'the people's right to subsistence will still be threatened in the event of social turmoil or other disasters'.

There is a marked difference in how China and the West see 'stability'. In Western minds, 'instability' connotes political mayhem, often followed by civil war. 'Instability' in Chinese thinking represents anarchy and in traditional lore brings great political misfortune. When the Chinese government speaks of 'instability' today, it does not have to mean actual social unrest and disturbance. References to 'instability' are often deployed in the context of ideological or political conflicts that would pass unnoticed in the West, where multi-party politics are accepted, and open, heated debate the norm. A principal difference between China and many other countries is that there remains only a very limited institutional framework allowing basic policies to be openly criticised. This does not mean that there are no conflicts – only that political disagreements among the elites are often shielded from public scrutiny.

China's perspective on rights and stability are shared by a number of Asian governments, including Singapore and Malaysia, who have been the strongest advocates of the view that developing countries may curtail civil and political rights in order to secure their economic and social well-being. Indeed, Singapore has been the most vocal in this debate. A consistent theme that has dominated political debate and shaped its trajectory since achieving independence in 1959 is its economic viability. The ruling People's Action Party (PAP), founded by senior minister Lee Kuan Yew, devised a strategy of economic development with government-backed industrialisation designed to attract foreign direct investment and to ensure that there was a diversification of economic activity. To achieve its goal, the PAP considered it essential to centralise state resources and power in the hands of the government through legislation. Thus, Singapore has one of the most state-directed economies in the world. Singapore also has extremely tough internal security laws that have enabled the government to detain a person without trial and without the executive having to produce substantial evidence against the detainees. These have often provoked international criticism. The government's approach is couched in terms of 'efficiency' to ensure political stability and harmony. The price that its people pay is the curtailment of some of the most fundamental rights and freedoms in the *UDHR*. This tiny city state has often been described as a state that best reflects a modern, successful state managed on 'Asian values' principles.

Such ideas inspired the controversial Bangkok Declaration, a draft declaration presented for debate by a number of Asian governments at the 1993 World Conference on Human Rights, in Vienna. The Bangkok Declaration was the culmination of a worldwide debate on 'Asian values'. As Asian countries have grown in economic strength and become economic powers, and while China also becomes a world political power, their leaders were able to argue that their continued advancement and success required stable politics and that Western-style adversarial politics was not a part of the Asian cultural tradition. It was also argued by some that Asian economies did so well in the 1980s and early 1990s because Asia had found an Asian model of development with strong governments. However, the 'Asian values' rhetoric subsided with the onslaught of the Asian financial crisis in 1997, as Asian economies and governments were shown to have vulnerabilities just like those in other parts of the world where financial regulation was weak. Nevertheless, the ideas underlying that debate remain influential.

China's starting point is the principle that rights are essentially domestic matters within state sovereignty, not subject to international interference.

Taiwan and Hong Kong

Taiwan and Hong Kong merit close study for anyone seeking to understand Chinese culture with respect to democracy and human rights. The peoples of Hong Kong and Taiwan are no less Chinese than the people of Mainland China. Historically, however, while they are both important parts of the modern history of China, the two regions have developed quite differently. Neither of them experienced communism in the 20th century, having to go through those painful ideological struggles where tradition must be denounced in favour of Marxism–Leninism–Maoism. Instead, Hong Kong and Taiwan provide examples of how these Chinese societies have cultivated strong, successful, independent civil institutions and environments of open political debate, which have not impeded their economic development. Hong Kong's per capita GDP is estimated at US$28,700 (2003) and Taiwan's is estimated at US$23,700 (2003), which are both higher than those for some European countries. For populations of seven million and 23 million respectively, their achievements are quite remarkable.

Taiwan

Taiwan politics is closely tied to its relations with Beijing. Beijing's policy is to reunify with Taiwan at the earliest opportunity, and its major concern today is that Taiwan is promoting independence by cultivating a separate Taiwan identity. The issue of maintaining peace across the Taiwan Strait is a major international concern. From Taiwan's perspective, it sees itself as having developed a society that is very different from Mainland China, and with a fully democratic political system in place. Reunification cannot take place until China, too, has a democratic system.

After the communists took over Mainland China in 1949, the nationalists (Kuomingtang – KMT) under Chiang Kai-Shek (1887–1975) moved the government of the Republic of China (ROC) to Taiwan in 1949. The KMT declared martial law and governed in a repressive manner, tolerating no dissent. With the death of Chiang, the presidency was passed on to his son, Chiang Ching-kuo (1910–1988), who in 1986 lifted martial law, revoked the ban on the formation of political parties, and allowed greater media freedom. From then on, Taiwan embarked on a period of political liberalisation that has gone further than any other Chinese society. The ruling party today, the Democratic Progressive Party (DPP), was formed in 1986 during the dying days of martial law. In 1996, the first presidential election was held on the basis of universal suffrage with a victory for the KMT. However, the DPP won the presidency in 2000 and again in 2004.

The 2004 presidential election provided electors with a choice of approaches from two parties on how to deal with Beijing, the most controversial issue in Taiwan politics, as well as testing Taiwan's young democratic system. A day before the election in March, the DPP candidate, Chen Shui-bian was slightly wounded by a bullet. The circumstances of what happened immediately became mired in controversy that led to much bitterness within the KMT, who accused the DPP of staging the shooting in order to swing votes in its favour. Chen narrowly won re-election the next day, but the KMT contested the results. The situation could have thrown Taiwan into a political crisis. Despite several rounds of protest by KMT supporters, the KMT's complaints were handled peacefully through the judicial system, resulting in a recount of the ballots. Chen's presidency was confirmed on 20 May, but the tension in fact had cooled long before the recount, as the people of Taiwan resumed their daily activities very quickly after the election. The underlying significance of this election was that it led to a marked rise in Taiwanese consciousness and public support for the island's progressive political programme of institutional and constitutional reform.

Hong Kong

Hong Kong people have had a full range of rights – with the notable exception of a democratically elected government – for a long time. Although Hong Kong is undoubtedly a Chinese city, and the vast majority of Hong Kong people are Chinese, the city has a distinctively Western liberal ethos. Hong Kong's civil and political atmosphere was shaped by 155 years of British occupation. For most of that time, the colonial government encouraged the pursuit of personal freedom in every area except politics. Rule of law in Britain's common law tradition established a stable civil society, and non-governmental organisations (NGOs) have multiplied and flourished, especially over the last two decades. A free media provided society with the platform for disseminating non-official ideas. The economy boomed with the government's *laissez-faire* philosophy.

Hong Kong's Legislative Council (LegCo) is constituted by election. However, the precise definition of what form that 'election' should take has been a major issue of contention – first between Britain and China, and now between Hong Kong and Beijing. During negotiations with the British, China maintained that some forms of appointment could qualify as elections. After extensive debate, China allowed Britain to open LegCo slowly to elections through two processes: direct election on the basis of universal suffrage on a geographical basis, and elections using functional constituencies as the base. Functional constituencies are special interest groups, such as banks, transport operators, corporate members of chambers of commerce, insurers, lawyers, doctors and teachers. The discussion in Hong Kong today is when and how it can proceed to directly electing its head of government as well as all the members of LegCo. Beijing has ruled out universal suffrage for the next round of elections for the chief executive in 2007 and LegCo in 2008. Nevertheless, public debate is continuing on reform for 2007–08 and beyond. This debate is about more than how to elect political leaders. It is about what kind of political system Hong Kong people think will best protect their rights and freedoms. Underlying that debate are Hong Kong's liberal values. Can the people maintain their values and systems within the People's Republic of China, with a political tradition that focuses more on state power than individual liberty?

Therefore, the real drama between Hong Kong and Taiwan and Beijing revolves around two opposing views of politics: between staying within orthodox political thinking and open debate that involves questioning fundamentals. Taiwan sees itself as a separate entity from Mainland China and as long as it is careful with the sensitive issue of independence, it wants to continue to develop its political culture as it sees fit. In the case of Hong Kong, which is a part of the People's Republic of China, Beijing's view on the pace and direction of the city's political development is, of course, critically important. While Beijing is trying to contain the discussion on political reform in Hong Kong within comfortable parameters, Hong Kong is questioning Beijing's assumptions in a manner that reflects its experience as a society that has enjoyed freedoms and the rule of law over several generations. Opinion surveys of Hong Kong attitudes show that people want their aspirations for democracy to be heard.

Thus, the clashes between Taiwan and Beijing, and Hong Kong and Beijing are not between Chinese and Western cultures but between different Chinese societies with different views about how society should be organised. Taiwan and Hong Kong have no doubt that they are Chinese societies. They have adopted ideas from elsewhere, which they have internalised for their own use, so that their people would be hard put to distinguish between such notions of liberty, rights and democracy and their own fundamental core values, irrespective of where and how those ideas may have first arisen.

The significance of Hong Kong being a part of the People's Republic, for Chinese political culture, is that it practises open, adversarial political debates and has more transparent decision-making processes than those of Mainland China. Questioning official assumptions, intentions and actions is considered healthy in Hong Kong, where alternative views are constantly being put forward. Since 1991, the election of a minority of LegCo's seats has helped to create a culture of political diversity. Civil society has grown over the years and independent NGOs play a significant role in advocating alternative ideas as well as calling the government to account for its failures. A free media provides society with the platform for disseminating non-official views and ideas. The uncensored internet helps to circulate information and ideas at lightning speed.

In Hong Kong, a number of very large but peaceful protests in 2003 and 2004 were seen as evidence of a mature and stable society. On each occasion people went back to work the following day and life proceeded as normal. In Beijing, the rallies were seen as a mark of potential instability and disunity. There lies the core of the current political impasse between Hong Kong and Beijing.

Up until the mid-1980s, Hong Kong people were often characterised as politically apathetic, with the roots of apathy arising from Confucian attitudes that ruled out upsetting authority. However, increased political interest began to surface as a direct consequence of the uncertainty over the Sino-British negotiations for the transfer of sovereignty to China in 1997. Even though Hong Kong has never been a democracy, its inhabitants have enjoyed personal freedoms and the rule of law. Once people become politicised, their political behaviour soon reflects a way of life where liberties are taken for granted. Signature campaigns, petitions, rallies, marches, protests, vigils, fasting for a cause, political commentaries and cartoons, conducting public opinion surveys, organising town hall gatherings, public fund-raising, and voting in elections have all become common political activities in Hong Kong.

As Mainland Chinese can now travel to Hong Kong more easily, Hong Kong has many surprises in store for them. Those who visited during the first week of June, will have witnessed Hong Kong's annual 4 June 1989 candlelight vigil commemorating Tiananmen, which remains a subject that still cannot be openly discussed on the Mainland. In 2004, over 80,000 people attended the vigil in Hong Kong. Press reports showed that Mainland visitors went to see what it was all about. A trip to the bookshops in Hong Kong will show a variety of publications about China that are unavailable on the Mainland. Mainlanders can buy reading materials that are *verboten* at home. Newspapers and magazines are full of all sorts of news and commentaries about the Mainland, including the controversy over political reform in Hong Kong, which are seldom reported nationally. Mainland visitors may also run into politicians standing on street corners raising money for campaigns or see NGOs organising events that are critical of government policies. The internet is not blocked in Hong Kong.

Conclusion

Societies that have a strong duty-based tradition, such as Hong Kong and Taiwan, or rights-based tradition, such as many Western countries, do not need to be seen to be in fundamental conflict. No civilised society is possible without the seeking of a balance between rights and responsibilities. The evolution of the human rights debate does not have to be seen as a conflict between Eastern and Western values either. Rather, it is a conversation between different Chinese societies as well as between Asian and Western societies, where new insights and ideas can and do emerge.

We have endeavoured to convey the ideological diversity throughout Mainland China, Hong Kong, Taiwan and Singapore at the same time as attempting to focus on the overarching forces, Confucianism and Liberalism, contributing to the evolution of Chinese human rights thought. The ideas of individualism and limited government have been adopted by Taiwan and Hong Kong, and their recent experiences have proven that multiparty systems are not inimical to Chinese civilisation. These experiences can be seen as experiments where the Chinese develop alternative governing systems to their state-centred tradition.

As the Mainland has already started to experiment with the election of village heads throughout the country, there are in fact many experiences arising from the region to learn from. Those experiences are very important in setting a constitutional agenda that can deal with the legitimate ordering of political life in the modern world. The two major questions are: how is the broadening of the political participation of ordinary citizens to be reconciled with enhancing the power and the legitimacy of the state; and how can open political debate and competition, as well as election be reconciled with creating good government? The challenge for Chinese civilisation is whether a modern Chinese state will eventually emerge on the Mainland that is not narrowly based and focused on doctrinaire central authority.

Thanks go to Kaitlyn Trigger for the initial research for this piece. Kaitlyn is a student at Yale University.

Endnotes

Samuel Huntingdon, *The Clash of Civilizations: Remaking of World Order*, Touchstone, Simon & Schuster, New York, 1997.

Ray Huang, *China: a Macro History*, revised with epilogue, M. E. Sharpe, New York, 1990.

Bruce J. Dickson, *Red Capitalists in China: The Party, Private Entrepreneurs, and Prospects for Political Change*, Cambridge University Press, UK, 2003.

Richard Baum, *Burying Mao: Chinese Politics in the Age of Deng Xiaoping*, Princeton University Press, 1994.

Stephen C. Angle, *Human Rights and Chinese Thought: A Cross-Cultural Inquiry*, Cambridge University Press, USA, 2002.

Joanne R. Bauer & Daniel Bell (eds), *The East Asian Challenge for Human Rights*, Cambridge University Press, USA, 1999.

Steve Tsang, *A Modern History of Hong Kong,* I. B. Taurus, London, 2004.

Philip A. Kuhn, *Origins of the Modern Chinese State,* Stanford University Press, USA, 2002.

Mao Zedong, 'Combat Liberalism', 7 September 1937, *Selected Works of Mao Tse-tung, Beijing Foreign Languages Press,* 1976, vol. II, pp. 31–33.

Human Rights in China, White Paper of the Chinese Government, 1991.

Contributors

Helena Kennedy is a barrister. She practises predominantly in the criminal law, but also undertakes judicial review, public inquiries and sex discrimination work. She is Chair of the Human Genetics Commission, a member of the World Bank Institute's External Advisory Council and was a member of the International Bar Association's Taskforce on Terrorism. A frequent broadcaster and journalist on law and women's rights, her award-winning book on women and criminal justice, *Eve Was Framed* was published in 1992. Her latest book *Just Law: The Changing Face of Justice – and Why It Matters to Us All* was published in March of this year. Her unique skills as an advocate and social reformer have taken her into many different fields of activity. From 1992 to 1997, she was chair of Charter 88, the constitutional reform group, which persuaded the new Labour government to make devolution and human rights legislation central planks of their manifesto. Helena was Chair of the British Council from 1998 to 2004.

Massoud Shadjareh is a founder member of the London-based Islamic Human Rights Commission (IHRC) and has chaired it since its inception in 1997. He is a veteran human rights activist, who first became interested in the field at university during anti-Vietnam war campaigns in the USA. After studying international relations, he turned to community development and anti-racism work. He is married to writer, researcher and fellow IHRC campaigner, Arzu Merali. The IHRC was founded as an 'independent, not-for-profit, campaign, research and advocacy organisation', deriving inspiration 'from the Qur'anic injunctions that command believers to rise up in defence of the oppressed'. Its work includes researching reports, monitoring the media, organising vigils, taking up discrimination cases, and campaigning for prisoners of faith. The IHRC is credited by the UN as a consultative body. Its website (*www.ihrc.org*) covers the main work of the organisation.

Heiner Bielefeldt was born in 1958 in Germany, near the Dutch and Belgium borders. He studied philosophy, history and theology in Bonn and Tübingen and received his PhD and Habilitation degrees in Philosophy. At the same time, he worked as a volunteer for Amnesty International and other human rights-related NGOs. In August 2003 he was appointed to the position of Director of the recently founded German Institute for Human Rights. Heiner Bielefeldt has written a number of books on philosophy of law, political ethics and philosophy of religion. His last book, *Symbolic Representation in Kant's Practical Philosophy* (Cambridge University Press) was published in 2003.

Christine Loh is the CEO of Civic Exchange, a Hong Kong-based not-for-profit think tank. Dr Loh is a lawyer by training but a commodities trader by profession. From 1992–97 and 1998–2000, she was a member of the Hong Kong Legislative Council. Among her achievements as a politician was initiating some historic legislation, including giving rural land inheritance rights to indigenous women, as well as creating a new law to protect Victoria Harbour from excessive reclamation. She did not seek re-election in 2000 choosing instead to found Civic Exchange, which is today the leading public policy think tank in Hong Kong. Today, Dr Loh is an analyst of Greater China politics and political economy, and is well-versed in urban planning and sustainable development. She writes extensively on these themes and has also anchored many radio and television public affairs programmes. She is a sought-after speaker internationally, and has received many awards.

Saad Halawani joined the British Council in September 2000, where he managed the Palestinian Rights Programme until 2003, Connecting Futures and the governance and society activities of the British Council. He has worked in curriculum development as a volunteer for the United Nations Volunteers Programme, where he developed human rights and conflict resolution curricula designed specifically to care for the needs of schoolgirls in marginalised communities. He completed his Master's degree from Birzeit University in Palestine in international studies, where he studied right-wing parties in Europe and their entry to parliaments, focusing on Austria, France, and the Netherlands. Saad has studied the history of Jerusalem and is a certified tour guide of the city.